Behind The Gate

A Holocaust Survivor's Journey
From Vilna To Tel-Aviv

By Michael Schemiavitz
Translated from Hebrew by Yossi L. Shem-Avi

Dedicated to the loving memory of:

My mother Chaya
My father Leib
My sister Lili
My grandmother Feiga Mera

❊

Who perished in the Holocaust

CONTENTS

PREFACE

Hundreds of diaries and memoirs have been written by holocaust survivors. Each story of survival is unique and the path to liberation was dissimilar from one to another. To escape from the hands of the murderers was an impossible mission and thus every story of survival implies a wonderous chain of events.

As I write these lines, I find myself wondering did this really happen to me? Is it possible that I experienced with my own flesh the hell's fire that gripped us during the duration of the German occupation?

I agreed to write my story after much encouragement and persuations by my wife and children. Unlike many survivor's families who wanted to protect their children, we shared some of our stories of the Holocuast with our children. Only later, studies validated our intuition that it was better for them to know then to be sheltered from it.

The relative short years of the war cannot ever be erased from my conscience and they follow me like a constant inseparable shadow. Despite that reality, the heavy load of those memories did not inhibit me from taking an active part in the fabric of life with dedication, loyalty and joy.

The past did not weaken my resolve, darken my spirit, nor impede my desire for life and renewal. It is not uncharacteristic for survivors to rehabilitate their lives, start families and thrust themselves into full productive existence.

In closing, I'd like to disclose that I did not seek the aid of any research tool while writing, and that the source of these words is my memory alone.

Michael Schemiavitz   February 2006
Tel-Aviv, Israel

INTRODUCTION FOR
THE ENGLISH EDITION

My father published his memoirs as we celebrated his eightieth birthday in Israel. His only wish for that event was to recreate his Bar Mitzvah and to be called to the Torah at his precious temple in Ramat Aviv, reading the same chapter Yithrro that he read 67 years before. The decision to translate the book to English was an easy one, wishing to share the story of the atrocities and survival with my own family, friends, colleages and the English readers at large.

I learned of some of the events told in this book for the first time during a 1993 visit to Vilna to commemorate the 50 year anniversary of its Ghetto's final extermination. Growing up, I knew very little about the war years of my father or my mother, herself an Auscwitz Concentration Camp surviver who shared her harrowing story as a young girl on video for the Shoah Foundation of Stephen Spielberg. I was keenly aware, however, of this vast and very dark cloud that covered my family's history and was constantly reminded of the Holocaust as it became an inseparable part of Israel's being. As I discover my parents history or read other personal testimonies and as I contemplate the events of World War II, I am struck by two opposite human traits; on the one hand the bottomless capacity for brutality and on the other the generosity of spirit and kindness that saved my parents and many others.

I always knew that Vilna - known in Jewish chronicles as "Jerusalem of the North" – was a special place and admired the spirit and distinct sweet Yiddish accent its survivors share. For almost 700 years, there has been a Jewish presence in Lithuania and the Litvaks became an integral part of its society, economy, culture, science and education. It has been estimated that of the 265,000 Jews living in Lithuania in June 1941, 254,000 or 95% were murdered or died during the war. At the start of the war, Vilna's Jewish population exceeded 75,000 and had over 100 synagogues, many Yeshivas and a thriving community, less then 5,000 survived.

The two years working on translating the book were very gratifying and brought me closer to my father, as we'd discuss various questions I had during my weekly Saturday calls to Israel. I am amazed how he was able to remember all the details, names and places, as if those powerful events were literally etched in his memory.

ACKNOWLEDGEMENTS

I'd like to thank the following people for their help and contribution. My sister Chaya Maor and niece Liron Perlmutter, who were instrumental in the Hebrew publication and who provided continuous advice. My wife Cathy Surratt who is my trusted partner, and my daughter Ella for her competent assistance. Deborah Bosley and Marty Settle for their insight and the title, and Dan Harris for his support.

Yossi L. Shem-Avi October 2008
Charlotte, North Carolina

INTRODUCTION

Michael's book is a unique and rare gem in the mosaic of memoirs of Holocaust survivors. The more testimonies are brought to light, the clearer picture is emerging of what happened there during the worst of time. Just as compelling is Michael's journey in Israel from its establishment to present day.

The story, through all its stages, is one of deep love to Israel and the Zionist cause, borne from a home steep in Jewish pride and hope for the future of the Jewish people and their aspirations to return to their homeland. Beginning with his Bar-Mitzvah's speech that was full of Zionist fervor, delivered in Hebrew, and throughout his life, Michael embodies the conviction that there is no other home for the Jews but in Israel.

I thank Michael for the privilege he gave all of us to share with his life's story and my personal gratitude for allowing me to share my thoughts that are a mere small beam to illuminate a larger source.

Winter 2006

Simcha Stein
Director
Ghetto Fighters Museum
Israel

Behind The Gate

Chapter 1

BEFORE THE TURBULANCE

I turned 13 in February 1939. I was called to the Torah, celebrating my Bar Mitzvah and reading from the *Ythrro* portion of the Torah at the Appatov synagogue on Portova Street in Vilna (Vilnious), the largest city in Lithuania (referred as Lita but was part of Poland at the time). Residing in that same building where I lived was the chief Rabbi of Vilna, Rubinstein, who was a member of the Polish Senate and a leader in the Mizrachi movement. My parents, my sister Lily, grandfather Meir Schochot, grandmother Feiga Meira, aunts, uncles and a large group of friends and neighbors were present at the service and the Kiddush following. In addition to the reading of the Torah and my Haftorah, I read in Hebrew a speech full of Zionist fervor that was received with support and adoration. Rabbi Rubinstein rose to the Bimah and congratulated me warmly on the occasion. It was a typical snowy winter in this northern city where temperatures regularly dipped below freezing. Schools would cancel only when it reached 13 below (Fahrenheit). The local radio would make the announcement of the closure while special flags were raised on tops of public buildings. We loved those free days and everyone would ice skate, glide on the snow and ski. Horse drawn snow carriages would carry people around making lovely and joyous ringing sounds with bells.

On many street corners, the city kept barrels with burning coal providing quick warmth for folks passing by – especially for the homeless. Our childhood's joy would occasionally turn sour when we were harassed by local bullies. Those juvenile anti-Semites tried to, and sometime succeeded in pushing and shoving us. Other times they yelled out cuss words and various humiliating remarks. For that reason, the Jewish kids typically tried to move about in groups. One of the popular epithets at the time was "Jews – leave us and go to Palestine." Ironically, to my friends and I who were mostly Zionists, that was a welcomed prophecy, as we dreamed and prayed to migrate to Israel where the Jewish presence had been growing since the turn of the Twentieth century.

I attended the Jewish elementary school, Tarbut, for the first six grades and then continued into high school at the same institution. The language spoken and taught was strictly Hebrew. We were steeped with the love of "Eretz Yisrael" (land of Israel) and Jewish pride. Tarbut in Vilna was the first Hebrew language school in the Diaspora and later hundreds opened across Poland. I spent ten years at the school and will always have wonderful memories of its teachers, fellow students and spirit. (The Tarbut building survived the war and now houses the Vilna Jewish Community offices and a Jewish museum; I visited the place several times recently and was overwhelmed with sweet memories of my early youth).

As spring arrived that year of 1939 we celebrated Passover, and in June school was let out. Our family, similar to most of our neighbors, vacationed in the surrounding areas that were rich with lakes, rivers, deep forests and potato fields. The future was promising and rosy as we enjoyed the nature that summer, fishing and picking wild berries in the vast forest.

I've always been interested in Polish and world politics. Before school, I would read the local Yiddish newspaper and would always keep my ears open to the adults discussing the events in Europe. When the Italians invaded Ethiopia in 1935 – what was known as the Second Italo-Abyssinian war – I knew the names of the Generals on both sides. During the Spanish Civil War, when General Franco fought the legitimate Spanish Republic, we, of course, supported the democratic regime, especially knowing that Franco was supported by the Italians and Germans. News about the increasing pressure on the German Jews by Hitler – that culminated in the famed "kristal nacht" in 1938, during which many Synagogues and Jewish institution were burned – brought anxiety and anger.

That same year the Germans annexed Austria, the *Ansschluss*, and early in 1939 following the Munich Agreement (known to the Czechs as the *Munich betrayal*), parts of Czechoslovakia (Sudetenland) were shamefully handed to Germany under the famed Chamberlain appeasement policy. Germany then pressured Poland to allow a geographic corridor connecting Eastern Prussia and Germany, but the Poles refused. Poland was swept by a wave of patriotism, including the Jewish population which strongly supported a strong stance against Nazi Germany. The Polish leadership fueled the illusion of a strong military that could defend against Germany. With the start of the war on September 1, 1939, Polish Calvary wielding bayonets were quickly defeated by a strong and modern German Army.

Needless to say, our summer vacation of 1939 was not relaxing and indeed turned to anxiety as, at the end August, we were told of the first draft of men, vehicles and horses. My father arrived from Vilna with the last bus available, planning to return us all home with a horse drawn carriage. That night, a fire broke out

3

in the barn of the farmer whose house we rented for the summer, claiming most of his possessions. Hundreds of local farmers volunteered to put the fire out by passing buckets of water from hand to hand, but to no avail.

That fire was a powerful symbol of what was next, and my parents, my sister and I returned to our apartment in Vilna very worried.

Soon after the German invasion of Poland, Great Britain and France declared war against Germany, honoring their mutual defense agreement with Poland, and by doing that made World War II a reality. The local civil defense instructed the town to dig trenches against bombardments, and at nights strict curfews were enforced. Vilna had many army units in its vicinity, and as the units mobilized, we, along with all the locals, followed them to the outskirts of town showering them with cigarettes, candy and flowers while singing patriotic songs. Many people swarmed the grocery stores to stock up on emergency food and supplies. Within days, there was no flour, sugar, salt or oil to be found. Abba, my mother's brother, was a grocer, and he made sure that our family was well stocked. The radio was full of marching band music and occasional secret Morse codes alerting the civil defense personnel of air strikes. I can still hear the dramatic voice of the announcer alerting before and after special messages. Rumors of the crushing defeat of the Polish Army by the Reich spread more panic among the Jewish population. We had little optimism about our fate, given the suffering of the German, Austrian and Czech Jews by the Nazis.

My father, who was a unit commander of the civil defense, made us so proud when he would put on his uniform. One evening, he asked me to go to the headquarters to fetch some literature for him. I carefully made my way through the dark streets when suddenly the lights lit and a truck driving by made a dramatic announcement that Hitler was assassinated during a coup. As I was digesting this shockingly good news, pandemonium broke out with soldiers and army vehicles moving in all directions. When I finally made it to the building, it was locked, and I discovered that the local army with the civil defense ran away towards the Lithuanian border because the Russian army was approaching Vilna. I ran home to the sound of artillery and for the rest of that night we sat in the basement. In the morning there was total silence. I ran outside and saw a large tank with a red star on it. The Soviet Union invasion of Vilna and the Eastern provinces of Poland came as a result of the Molotov-Ribbentrop pact that Stalin and Hitler agreed to as their non-aggressive resolution.

*Grandfather Michael, Grandmother Leah Golda
and Leib Schemiavitz*

Leib Schemiavitz in a photo sent to the US from Shirvint

Michael's mother Chaya and her brother Abba

Vilna 1929. on the right: Uncle Yitzhak, standing behind his daughter Sonya, center: uncle Yirmiyahou and his wife Sonya guests on the left

Chapter 2

SOVIET RULE AND INDEPENDENT LITA

The Jewish population was relieved; there was no immediate danger for our survival.

The might of the Soviet Army was very impressive. For the first time we saw full size tanks with long-range artillery cannons hauled by heavy trucks and many soldiers marching day and night. Their presence was evident in every street corner. We had the chance to meet Jewish officers of the Red Army – some of whom were high ranking, including Generals. This was a refreshing phenomenon in comparison to the Polish Army which did not allow Jewish soldiers to become commissioned officers.

Since the schools were all closed at the start of the hostilities, we enjoyed leisurely life of movies and play. The Red Army provided entertainment in the city parks with marching bands and dance troupes. My parents did not share my generation's carefree life and optimism. They were reserved and very critical of the Soviet rule, knowing that it was only a matter of time before they would nationalize businesses, limit personal freedom, censor free speech, outlaw Jewish organizations and disturb the Synagogues and other religious activities. Red Army officers bought clothes and shoes, and soon most stores were empty. Food supply in the city collapsed with the need to feed the Army. This situation continued until October, when the Soviet Union declared an agreement with the local government to transfer the sovereignty of Vilna and its vicinity to the Lithuanians with the Red Army's access to military bases.

For the first time in 20 years, Vilna was independent again – losing independence in 1919 under the Polish occupation. Slowly, life became normal with schools opening and commerce showing signs of life again. As Vilna was declared the new Capitol, many civil servants and bureaucrats had to move back from Kovno and needed apartments. The city's landlords, especially owners of apartment buildings in affluent areas, realized the windfall. Stores were full again with local products of fish, grain, dairy and meat.

The demographic structure was such that ethnic Lithuanians were a minority of several thousands, a majority of Poles and 80,000 Jews comprising about 40% of the total population (including Jews that fled from German soil). Tarbut School reopened with similar structure and the same teachers, with one notable difference – the Polish language and history gave way to Lithuanian heritage. The total isolation of Vilna from the rest of Lita for twenty years took a toll on the connection between the two separate Jewish communities. With the opening of the borders came an influx of relatives that we hadn't seen in many years. One memorable event was my grandfather Meir's brother, Rabbi Avram Druskeivitz who came, unfortunately, one month after his brother's passing. Our house became the center of activities with both of my parents receiving many relatives enjoying the new freedom of movement.

Along with the stream of refugees that arrived in Vilna from the German occupied territories, came variety of Jewish youth groups and Yeshiva students. The efficiency with which so many displaced persons were absorbed was a testament to the leadership of the Vilna Jewish community. Many years later, after the war, I occasionally met some of those refugees that stayed in Vilna, all of whom were very grateful to the Vilna Jews and their hospitality. Among the new arrivals were my uncle Yitzchak Yaacov Schemiavitz, his wife Liza, and his daughter Fanya with her husband Aaron Noovinsky, their nine month old Miriam and three older children Genya, Fella and David. The entire family was housed at my father's older brother Yirmiyahou Shlomo Schemiavitz's who had a large apartment of seven bedrooms. Many Jews took advantage of the new State status of Lithuania and its ability to issue Visas and migrated to Israel, North and South America. In our own apartment we hosted two families sponsored by a relief organization and enjoyed supper together on Shabbat evenings.

Vilna was enjoying its new place as a major city, unlike its provincial status during the Polish Administration. Commerce and small industry flourished along with a real estate boom. Strong demand for housing, propelled by population growth and the arrival of government offices from Kovno and foreign embassies, filled our apartment building at the center of town. Among the renters were military and police officers, senior officials and their families. The Baltic States, including Lita, enjoyed relative calm and prosperity while the rest of Europe was already engulfed in war. Still, many of the uprooted Jews wanted to leave, but where would they go, how would they pay for the trip and who would grant them a Visa? One example of a heroic and unselfish act was that of the Japanese Consulate General in Vilna who took it upon himself to issue thousands of Visas for Jews to travel to Japan. When discovered by the Japanese government, he was fired and dishonored.

The new independent Lithuanian regime survived a mere eight months. In May 1940 the Soviets sent an ultimatum demanding the extradition of those who killed soldiers of the Red Army. Within 24 hours, Soviet forces left their bases and quickly took control of the country. The leadership, including the President, fled abroad. Similar scenarios took place in the neighboring Baltic States of Latvia and Estonia. With control over the entire Baltic region, the Soviets established local militias and conducted a referendum on the issue of joining the "Socialist Family of Nations." This, of course, was a fraud with 100% voting in favor of joining. Now, with Vilna being part of the Soviet Union, the situation regressed once again with the immediate effect of nationalizing private property. All political activities, except Communism, were banned. Hebrew was declared a reactionary language and was not allowed to be used in school. Our school switched to Yiddish and had to use the Communist curriculum. The condition of our Gentile neighbors who held key positions in the Lithuanian administration was desperate. Officers in the security forces were among the many that were fired. Their elegant wives had to get menial jobs to survive and many lost their apartments that were needed for the Soviet officers. My parents did their best for their neighbors, providing meals and even small loans. Some trusted us with their most precious belongings and asked us to hide them so that the Soviets would not confiscate them. These small acts of kindness by my parents later proved to save our lives!

The Soviet rule quickly brought about the nationalization of private property which included my family's large apartment building where we all lived. My father, using personal contacts, was able to get a job as a property manager for another building that was taken by the State. Landing a job was critical for survival during that period, and we all felt a relief following the loss of our building.

The Regime was not kind to any groups they deemed hostile which included: unproductive persons, wealthy property owners, Zionists and ultra-orthodox Jews. Conversely, Jews with past communist leanings – especially those who took part in the pre-Revolutionary underground – were rewarded with high level jobs in the Soviet bureaucracy. Owners of large dwellings, such as my parents, were forced to take in families in need of housing, and we did.

Despite the economic uncertainty, the unpredictable arrests and transfers to Siberia, the majority of the Jewish community felt that they were much better off then under German occupation. Symbolizing this sentiment, I remember a well known merchant, Beztalel Noose, who declared, as he was being forced out of Vilna to Siberia: " Don't feel sorry for me fellow Jews, I prefer giving Stalin the keys [to his business that was nationalized] then my head to Hitler." That same year, 1940, the community lost Rabbi Chaim Ozer Groodzinsky – a major figure in the Jewish community who was revered as a righteous man who touched many lives with his wisdom and humility. Thousands came to his funeral including, some say, Communists who wanted to pay their respect.

I was influenced heavily by the Communist propaganda that preached world solidarity, declared anti-Semitism illegal and allowed Jews admittance to higher education. Like my peers, I enjoyed the free cultural events that the State provided. In comparison to the vitriol atmosphere and anti-Semitic burst under the Poles and Lithuanians, we appreciated the relative calm. The older generation was more cautious and feared what was coming. The prediction was that the Soviets would harden their treatment of the Jews and would eventually arrest or extricate us from Vilna.

Wealthy merchants, large property owners, Zionist activists and criminals were deemed not suited to live in sensitive border areas and were regarded as enemies of the State. Indeed, in May 1941 the NKVD (Soviet secret police) combed Vilna and exiled many Jews, Poles and local Lithuanians that were deemed as one the aforementioned groups to remote Russian territories. Many people I knew who felt uncertain about their status hid until the storm passed, but my family survived that period unscathed.

Chapter 3

JUNE 1941, THE GERMAN OCCUPATION

In June of 1941 school was out for summer vacation. Everyone was preparing for their vacations in one of the many resorts in the Baltic. Thousands of youth were swimming in the river Vilia that crossed the city while rich lilac aroma intoxicated everyone. Our class made the final preparations for our trip up river on a steam boat to the town of Vorky that was scheduled for Sunday, June 22. I got up early filled with anticipation and was happy to see that the sun was shining. I looked out the window and noticed unusual military movement. Soon, sirens followed and we all hoped that this was only a drill. It was not. Luftwaffe aircrafts were bombing our city. One bomb fell close to our house and we lost some windows. There was no doubt, we were in a war. An official announcement from Prime Minister Molotov at noon declared that Germany was attacking the Soviet Union. Fear took over us as we watched the Red Army retreating while local underground militias were firing shots at their backs. During the night of June 24, advanced units of the German Army entered Vilna.

With the windows shut and the front gate to the building locked, we sat in the apartment alert and frightened. We had two visitors that day. First was the building doorman who would normally bow his head and lower his hat at the sight of my parents. Not this time. He broke into out apartment and offered to protect us if we paid him money. He also pointed at an antique wood framed full-length mirror and asked for it. My parents were furious and threw him out. He promised to return and reminded us that the life and property of Jews were worthless. We quickly realized how right he was. The second visit was my uncle Yirmiyhou. "Leibe" he told my father, "Now that the Soviets are gone, the Germans will return Lithuania's independence, and we need to prepare to get our property back and start to collect rent." My father, his younger brother, mocked him and said that this was not the Germany of the First World War who treated Jews respectfully (Jews fought for Germany in WWI). "We're facing," he said, "Very tough times."

The German Army demanded that those with private spacious homes would house officers. Thus, two of our apartment rooms were taken by three officers of the Wehrmacht.

They were polite and, ironically, their presence provided us with security against the random and frequent crimes committed daily by local thugs, which included breaking into Jewish homes in broad daylight, stealing, raping and murdering. Our lives had indeed become worthless. Soon after the German officers left, the gate keeper returned with more nerve and took from us anything he wanted. Locals wearing no uniforms except a white ribbon across their chests began kidnapping Jewish males. We dubbed them "Chapunes." In one of their raids, they came toward our house and I ran to a Lithuanian lady neighbor who allowed me to hide in her bathroom. Minutes later, I heard the Chapunes asking her if she was hiding anyone. My heart was pounding as she calmly and politely told them that as a concerned citizen it was her duty to cooperate and she would never hide a wanted person. I heard the door shut. They left and I was able to return home.

What happened to the hundreds who were kidnapped? First, we heard rumors that the militia sent them to a work camp in the German occupied territories; few letters arrived to the families of the victims that confirmed their wellbeing. Soon though, we heard from a few Poles who lived just outside the Ponar Forest that they witnessed a daily routine of Jewish men being pushed toward the Ponar and being shot in mass grave. Of course no one believed this to be true and we speculated that it was a vicious propaganda to spread fear among us. Even the most pessimistic among us did not think it was conceivable for the Germans and the Lithuanian Militia to murder Jews in the forest just because they were Jewish. Coming to that sad realization took a few more years and many more dead.

Former officers of the Lithuanian security forces happily joined the German effort as fighting officers or in administrative jobs. Now that we were desperate, we turned to our neighbors that we knew for years for help. One day my uncle Yimiyahou was kidnapped and was taken to the local jail. We asked a wife of a Lithuanian officer who worked for the Germans to ask for his release. She agreed, but unfortunately, as she was walking towards his office, she was struck by a piece of broken glass and had to be taken to the emergency room. My mother stood every day for hours outside the jail's main entrance waiting for my uncle to come out. A few days later, the gate opened and she saw him among a large group of men. She ran towards him with a basket of food and was immediately hit in the head by the butt of a soldier's gun. He then took her into the Police station and forced her to mop all the floors in the bathrooms. We sat at home waiting for hours, and finally Mother came back exhausted and humiliated.

The German occupation demanded that the Jewish community find and commit men for work projects. My father Leib received an order to report to the Gestapo offices on Mitzkevitz Street. That building was the court house under the Polish regime. A group of men, including my dad, was sent to a location close to our house to clean and do simple repair jobs. He came back late on that first day tired and depressed. He told us that when he was unable to lift a wheelbarrow full of building material, a German supervisor hit him and proceeded to show him how to do it right. He too, though much younger, was unable to pick up the wheelbarrow.

One of our neighbors, Mr. Kemermacher, a well to do merchant of tires, motorcycles and the operator of a bus line, as well as a close friend of the family, was among the group my father worked with at the Gestapo HQ. He became their supervisor and gained special status because of his fluent German and his credentials as a supporter of the German Army during WWI. (Later, I'll tell the unusual story of his activities under the German occupation.)

At the beginning of September 1941, the first rumors of the German intent to create a Jewish Ghetto began to circulate. We didn't think at that particular time that this was entirely negative, as our lives became unbearable with daily incidents of attacks, theft, murders and extortions.

Vilna's German Governor published an edict with a demand of 5,000,000 Rubles as a ransom for the city's Jewry. He would accept cash and/or jewelry and furs. He further demanded that our community leaders would be responsible for the collection. We were given 48 hours to come up with the ransom. They took sixteen of our community leaders as hostages with the threat that they would be executed unless the ransom materialized. Our leaders pleaded in vein to extend the impossible deadline. At the close of the 48 hour period, a delegation brought in about half of the amount demanded. The sixteen hostages and the delegation that brought the money were immediately killed.

Soon following this event, during the night of August 31, we heard horrific screams from the streets. We found out in the morning that five thousands Jews – whole families including children – were taken to jail at Lukishki. The German Army distributed propaganda posters accusing our community of instigating violence and killing their soldiers. This was later known as the "great provocation" which was a complete fabrication and was designed as a precursor to the coming move towards the Ghetto. Indeed, on the 6th of September 1941, the Germans began herding Jews into the old Jewish quarter that was already experiencing high density.

Chapter 4

THE JEWISH GHETTO IN VILNA

We were finally all taken to the Ghetto. Father left early to work at the Gestapo's headquarters and Mother and my Grandmother were left helpless. My sister Lili was crying endlessly, picking up on the general anxiety. I was left, being 15 and the remaining "man" in the house, to pack quickly. I spread sheets on and floor and filled them with whatever items came to mind. We left most our possessions with a young Lithuanian lady who rented a room from us and became part of the family. Each one of us dressed with several layers and with our hand full of towels, sheets and extra personal belongings. We gathered in the courtyard awaiting the local police. I remember it being a sunny and warm day and feeling cumbersome with the extra layers of clothes.

As the local officers arrived, we gathered like a herd, feeling depressed, frightened and humiliated. Lovely music wafted through the window of one of our gentile neighbors. A dear friend of our family whose husband was an officer came down with us and asked the officer in charge to spare us and take our family only to the Ghetto. I spoke Lithuanian and understood her request but found it very odd. Of course to the Ghetto, where else? Our house was approximately three kilometers from the entrance to the old Jewish neighborhood that was declared now as the Ghetto into which all of Vilna's Jewish population was now crammed. The journey was slow and chaotic with thousands of families including children and elderly carrying their possessions and layers of clothes. To my surprise, we were spared abuse except for verbal. As we progressed, we were joined by more families coming out of every house and street corner, forming a human river of desperate people marching into the unknown. The stream of people became larger as we approached the gates of the Ghetto. The crowd was pushing and shoving; children were screaming, looking for lost parents as parents were frantically searching for their kids. The crowd was halted as we arrived at Zavalna Street and slowly we entered through the guarded gates of the Ghetto. We were surrounded by the local police and SS officers and our family with many others entered a courtyard in Rodnicka Street. We forced ourselves into a very crowded apartment with dozens of inhabitants. In the kitchen with a single faucet, a long line of thirsty people waited for a drink of water. The bathroom commode was overfilled and stench was everywhere. We were lucky, because as more families arrived, they were forced to squat in the stairwells and still others were left outside altogether; it was just too crowded. Going to the public bathroom outside was a major task that took time and determination as you trampled over the crowded stairwell and the streets. Was it possible that only the day before we had our own spacious apartment with the privacy of our own washroom? How could we live in this filthy unfamiliar space with so many people?

Our misery was compounded by the terrible fear we felt for the fate of Dad. After a sleepless night I ventured outside seeking some information. I ran into a friend from school who told me that most of the families from my neighborhood were taken to the Lookishki prison and from there to Ponar for execution – he was able to escape in the chaos. I then understood the comment that our neighbor made to the officer the day before and how she saved our lives. I was terrified for my Dad who could now be in route to Ponar or worse, already there. Not able to find Dad or additional information about him, I enlisted to work at the Judenrat office at 6 Rodnitski Street. I joined a group of 500 and together we were taken to a warehouse district close to the main train station.

Our task was to transfer, using our hands alone, bags of cement, each weighing 50kg, to waiting freight cars a few hundred yards away. It was difficult to breathe or see being inside a cloud of cement, but at gun point and with constant threats by German soldiers, we had to keep moving. After five hours and being close to exhaustion we had a break with hard crackers and frozen fish that I couldn't eat. After five more hours we were done for the day. The next day I recognized a friend of my family who I knew was working with my Dad at the Gestapo building. He told me that like him, my Dad escaped and joined the Jews that were taken to Ghetto number two on the other side of town. About 12,000 people were taken to this part of the city that was mostly empty following the extermination of its inhabitants at Ponar in a mass grave earlier. Our friend told my Father that my Mother, Grandmother, sister and I were in Ghetto number one and in few days, my Dad was able to join us. The reunion was very emotional and lifted our spirits; especially my mother's who was very upset. Dad brought his brother Yitzhak Yaakov, his wife Liza, and their children David, Sonia and Genya to our space that already had forty inhabitants. Fanya, another daughter, with her two year old girl Miriam, found refuge with a Polish group in the forest.

My Father and I were able to join a labor group that was assigned to work at a German Army maintenance facility. It was fortunate that Dad had a lot of experience in light maintenance and repair, having been a property Manager of the family's real estate. I did mostly cleaning work and stalking the furnaces. The work and condition was relatively easy, and we were given bread and soup to eat. We were also able to bribe Polish workers with money and garments to give us extra food which we snuck into the Ghetto to feed the family. Another day we concealed under our coats few pieces of wood that we later used to cook potato soup. The ration in the Ghetto was that of starvation – 1/2kg (about one pound) of bread per person per week. The bread was consumed immediately when distributed.

On Yom Kippur, October 1, 1941 we went to work as usual – we had no choice – but not a person in the whole group touched the broth they gave us for lunch. The fact that we fasted was perceived as an act of provocation by our guards, but for us was a source of momentary pride and solidarity. We returned to the Ghetto that evening, tired and hungry, just in time for the "Ne'ila," the closing prayer of the holiest day of the year. There were thousands of worshippers at the filled synagogue and many more outside. Instead of prayer and song, one could hear crying and communal despair from a community in total fear that begun to mourn itself. Later that night we heard gun shots and screaming from adjacent apartments. Quickly the rumors spread that the Germans, with the help of local Lithuanian Militia, were evacuating whole families toward the gates of the Ghetto. All of us crowded into the attic, shoving anything we could find against the door. We stayed awake and on guard all night. In the morning the streets were quiet, and Dad and I returned to work.

In the "action" of that Yom Kippur, 4,000 Jews from both Ghet-to number one and two were taken to Ponar and quickly shot to death into a mass grave. This "action" shook us to the core as we shed any illusions of hope that we would be left to live in the Ghetto – despite its horrific conditions. Those of us with working permits mistakenly thought that that piece of paper would save us. We heard that during the "action" German soldiers tore to pieces work documents shown to them by some of those taken to Ponar.

Chapter 5

DOCUMENTION – LICENSE TO LIVE

At this point, everyone in the Ghetto felt completely helpless and uncertain of the future. The Germans tried to create an illusion that the Jews who were deemed essential to the war effort – those with skills who were young adults and able – would be treated differently than the old, feeble and useless, including children and women. Furthermore, they explained that past killings of those holding work permits was a clerical misunderstanding. To avoid such mistakes they announced that new yellow work permits with "Specialist," or *FACH ARBEITER*, would be issued, allowing its owner to also register their wife and two children under the age of sixteen. The administration issued 3,000 permits, 1,000 of which were assigned to a fur factory, several hundred to tool shops inside the Ghetto and the remaining to be divided among other unknown destinations.

This cynical and cruel plan detailed that only permit holders, each with three companions, totaling 12,000 people would be allowed to live. Those with more than two children, or those having children older then sixteen were asked to make an impossible selection of whom to include with the family list – which meant that a parent had to make an unspeakable choice of which of their children would live or die. This was a tragedy difficult to comprehend, and it signaled how intent the Germans were to torture our defenseless people both physically and psychologically. Everyone was now focused on getting the coveted permits. Those with money offered huge sums to supervisors in the designated work places in order to be asked to work there. Young, single men with permits had to choose between many women ready to marry quickly – those with money and beauty stood a better chance. Others, with no children and good chances for the permit, had to choose which children to adopt in order to save them, facing many desperate, pleading parents.

The place where Dad worked had 80 Jews and only eight permits allocated. We knew that having neither specific skill nor cash with which to bribe, he had no chance to be chosen, and we accepted our fate. On October 15, 1941 work places began to hand out permits. At Dad's location, the German supervisor called all the workers for a line-up, and he heard his name – Leib Schemiavitz – called. The Officer beat him severely and after few minutes gave him a yellow work permit. When he got home, beaten up, he showed us the document. How did this miracle happen and why was he beaten? He discovered later from the leader of the group that a lady, who was the manager of the German Labor office – *ARBEIT AMT* – and was handling the issuance of the permits, was the wife of a high ranking Lithuanian officer who lived at our apartment building. They remembered that during the Soviet rule my Dad protected them from eviction and when she saw his name among those not chosen to work she insisted on including him with the workers despite the vehement objection of a German supervisor.

Shortly following, the Ghetto's police announced that permit holders with their wives and two children needed to report to the police station to get ID cards for their three allowed companions. It was late in the day when we got there and I will never forget that night. Thousands of people blocked the entrance to the station begging those with permits to take their children. There was chaos and madness, pushing and shoving and my father kept his permit very deep inside his pocket. Among the pandemonium, parents lost their children. One could hear the screams of desperate parents calling their children's names and kids panicking looking for parents. My sister and I clutched tightly to our parents hands, and as we made our way forward we were beaten repeatedly by German officers. It was dawn by the time we got the ID cards. Later we were told to report to Dad's work location, and we decided to attempt to smuggle my grandmother with us. Gestapo soldiers stood at the entrance of the building and we marched Dad first then my mom, my sister, grandmother and me last. A soldier grabbed my grandmother and I and told us we couldn't join the rest. My Dad pleaded with him to let me go since I had the ID. While another family tried to escape, causing the soldier to turn, Dad grabbed my hand and the four of us left, leaving my grandmother behind. We never saw her again and I am certain that she was taken to Ponar and was killed there into the mass grave.

The work camp was located a few kilometers outside the city. We found ourselves with other families who also held permits in a simple cabin with wood beds, running water and most importantly wood furnace. We stayed in the cabin for three days and heard rumors of another Ghetto cleansing and deportation to Ponar. When we returned, the situation in the Ghetto was different. We discovered that during the three days in the camp, thousands who were left behind were taken to Ponar to be killed. We were given a larger apartment with fewer people than we had before and later found many Jews who survived in hiding places. To be with a permit or an ID meant that you belonged to a privileged group and the rest, with no permits, were illegal. We allowed several families with no permits to share our space but there was constant tension and fear of being caught. There was also haggling over water and kitchen use time with those holding permits demanding better priorities. However, I know of no instances where anyone without permit was turned in to the authorities.

Chapter 6

1942 - STABILITY IN THE GHETTO

Our three bedroom apartment faced Zavalna Street and though the windows were boarded up, I could see the street outside the Ghetto through the cracks. Eight of us shared a room: my parents, my sister and I, my cousins Sonya and Genya, a refugee from Poland named Dov Griener, and his ten year old daughter Rachel. The room next door housed the Hoffmans including their daughter-in-law and their three year old grandson (their son was kidnapped and disappeared earlier) and a couple named Reuven and Tova Mishkovski with their thirteen year old son Kalman. In the largest room were the owners of the apartment who survived the expulsion from the Ghetto by hiding in the attic. They were: the mother Rivka Pesker, her daughter Shifra Weiner with her fifteen year old son Toula (her husband was killed during one of the provocations). With them were also the Rottenbers numbering four and three surviving sons of the Lunski family. There was also a woman named Grunia and her daughter Genya in the attic.

Our diet consisted mostly of boiling water with drops of rye flour and potato skins and an occasional slice of bread, which was difficult to obtain. We had to burn small logs of wood in the kitchen to heat the water and the smoke billowing was so bad that the occupants of the attic had to come down. Grunia who could pass for a local peasant girl would sneak out and bring us food she bagged from villagers in the surrounding area outside the Ghetto.

We suffered little provocation during that relative calm of 1942. My Dad and I would leave for work, he at a local paper mill formally owned by a Jewish family and me in a repair shop for locomotives at the train station. Mother worked at the laundry and Lily stayed to clean the apartment. During that and other calm periods, the Jewish community organized some educational and cultural activities for children trying to maintain some measure of normalcy and to keep the children occupied. Lily, too, participated in some of the classes.

My uncle Abba – my mother's brother – with his wife Feiga and their only daughter Sara, lived in Bezdany, about 35 kilometers from Vilna. Like many other work camps close to the thick spruce forest, it was dedicated to producing logs for heating and had about 300 Jews. The laborers were allowed to enter Vilna every other week and we waited anxiously for my uncle who walked that distance on foot to bring us country bread, potatoes and occasionally vegetables. During one visit he was able to bring few logs of wood which became very scarce inside the city. He got sick during one visit with high fever and in the hospital was diagnosed with pneumonia. In few weeks he got better and was ready to get back to his camp and family. At that period my parents were terribly worried about the condition of my sister Lily. She was extremely thin and frail. My uncle offered to take her with him to Bezdany thinking that the country air and better nutrition might improve her condition. After much agonizing, they decided to let Lily go with Abba.

With thousands of people going in and out of the Ghetto to work, despite the prohibition of transferring any food items into the

Ghetto, it became quite common for many to smuggle ingredients in many creative ways. I'm not aware during that year of anyone dying of hunger, as many had in other Ghettos that were hermetically closed. The routine at the end of the work day was to go through a long inspection line by the German police, the local police and the Ghetto's police. Almost every worker was frisked, but the punishment for basic ingredients like flour and potatoes was only a beating and occasionally being taken to the station for few days. When the police chief Frantz Murer showed up, the punishment was more severe, as was the case when the singer Lubba Levitzki was taken to the Gestapo station and shot when he caught her with oats.

The workers became very clever in ways to smuggle food into the Ghetto. Everyone had sewed liners inside their coats and would bring in potatoes and flour. Inside hats we had small compartments to put slices of bread when we could find them. Tradesmen who had tool boxes fabricated double compartments to hide food. I obtained such a tool box from a relative who was guarding the gate with the Jewish police (the Germans installed a Jewish administration inside the Ghetto to run the day to day needs of the community, including the police). To this day, the survivors of the Vilna Ghetto remember with much hate, the sadistic Jewish cop, Laves, who was in charge of the gate to the Ghetto that cooperated with the Germans and locals. One evening, when I returned to the Ghetto and tried to enter the gate, Police Chief Murer was there, and the whole group was taken to a large room and was stripped naked – men and women alike. The police inspected every garment and those who refused to strip were brutally beaten. The purpose of the search was to find jewelry and watches. After they took every ring, necklace and earring we were thrown back to the street, cold and humiliated.

The train maintenance facility where I worked was managed by the Reichs Bahn (train management) and the person assigned to watch over the Jews was a short German called Jacob Rauber. His nickname was "king of the Jews" because he did not have typical Aryan features and was at times kind to us and sensitive to our needs. Yet at other occasions, he demonstrated quick temper and a mean streak. Our own leader was Tuvia Sheres, a brother of a class-mate of mine, who was regarded as brave, proud and fearless. The Germans regarded him as industrious and valuable and to us he was a loyal and trusted friend. He was able to bribe Rauber with a ring bearing his own initials to escort us into and out of the Ghetto. This was very comforting, as there were many instances that local militia and Germans would harass, kidnap and even kill laborers.

Our group's chores included cleaning the station and the trains, loading and unloading merchandise, and replenishing coal. Occasionally, we would unload a car with potatoes or cabbage and we would stash and then smuggle as much as we could back to the Ghetto. In the winter, our main chore was to clear the snow from the tracks and roads leading to the station. We took our lunch break, which consisted of a bowl of broth, in the main mess hall along with the other laborers who were mostly Poles and Lithu-anians. Of course, we were the last in line to eat and were given what was left. Occasionally, we would eat at the dining room re-served for the Germans and the food there was tasty and nutritious. The Foremen were older, experienced "Meisters" who treated everyone according to their work ethics and ability. It was such a relief, though temporary, to be treated with some degree of respect and to feel like human by another person. Only a few of these civilian supervisors exhibited abuse both verbal and physical.

Every day we witnessed eastbound trains carrying thousands of German soldiers and military equipment heading to fight the Red Army. They would peek through the windows, and when they saw the yellow star stitched to our coats, verbal abuse and laughter would ensue. Quietly, we wished them to return west in caskets covered by the German flag. Later, we saw trains returning Westbound with thousands of wounded Germans and that sight brought us such joy and hope. We realized for the first time that the Wehrmact was confronted by a tough Red Army and this was not a walk in the park by any measure.

The engineers piloting the trains were not Germans but of other European nationalities. They shared with us information from the front, specifically incidents of rail tracks being sabotaged by bands of "Partisans." (These Partisans who escaped from Ghettos, camps and other hardships, survived deep in the forests for years in some cases. Some of these groups that obtained weapons – and in some cases received material assistance from the Red Army – dedicated themselves to cause damage and destruction to the German Army.) Quite frequently, we witnessed the search and rescue train that was parked at our facility depot on missions to sites of rail bombings by the Partisans. When that happened, we rejoiced that someone was able to cause harm to the people who were dedicated to destroying our nation.

We were not the only ones to suffer from the German brutality. They reserved an extra measure of sadistic pleasure for the Red Army's POW's. In addition to harsh labor conditions, they prevented them from medical attention, starved them and allowed little water. We heard horrific screams for help from trains returning from the front filled with Soviet prisoners, begging for food and water. Despite our meager condition, we would risk being punished and would toss pieces of bread to them.

The station was a major rail hub that brought train crews from all over Europe. The more stories we heard about how daring the Partisans were against the Germans, the more we began to dream of an escape to join one of the bands hiding in one of the cars. Over the months, we met many conductors and other crew members who told us in some detail about the whereabouts of the Partisans and their movements. We also traded anything we could find for food, including clothes, pins and soap. I befriended a very kind and sensitive Pole and over a period of several months saw him frequently and earned his trust. He updated me about the fighting in the Eastern front and the heavy casualties the Germans were suffering by the Red Army. He also knew a great deal about the Partisans, their courageous attacks and survival skills in the deep forests. I mastered the courage to finally ask him if he would hide me on his outbound train and drop me at the edge off the forest where I could join them. He refused, citing the danger and the fact that he did not trust the discretion of his crew.

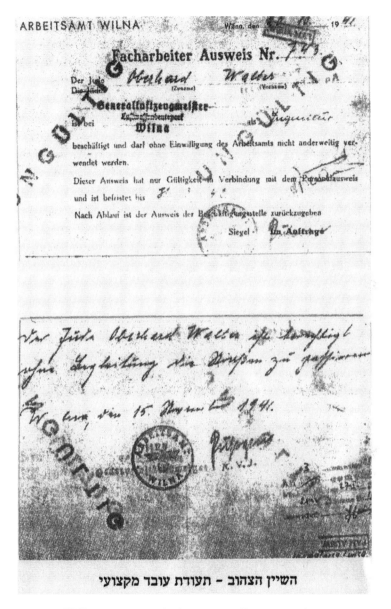

השיין הצהוב – תעודת עובד מקצועי

Yellow tag – work document. License to live.

List of Ghetto's population dated May 1942. The Schemiavitz family is listed lines 57,58,81,82 Michael's name is number 83

Chapter 7

THE BURNING OF THE BEZADNI'S JEWS

It was a Saturday in July of 1943 when I met a conductor who told me about the extermination of the Bezadni work camp. All the Jews at the camp, he said, were locked inside the barracks and burned alive. That was the camp where we sent my sister Lily to be with my uncle Abba and his family because of the deteriorating conditions in our Ghetto. That very same Saturday, we had expected with much anticipation a visit from my uncle who promised to bring Lily along. All week we were so excited to see Lily again. Was it possible that this horrible story could be true – that instead of a joyous reunion we'd begin to mourn for her? I could not face going back to the Ghetto to share this story with my parents. I collapsed in a corner and cried, completely broken down. When I finally returned to the Ghetto, the rumor had already spread about the fate of the Bezadni Jews. Together with my parents, we spent the night crying for my sister Lily. Most painful was to watch my Dad who was crazy about his little girl. It was he who opposed sending her with his brother to the camp initially, and now he blamed himself for not standing firm with his intuition and allowing her to leave the house.

The next day, additional rumors circulated about children who left the camp before the extermination to collect berries and mushrooms at nearby fields. A sliver of hope that Lily was among them and would return soon dimmed in time. We never saw her again. For years after the end of the war I kept hoping that I would find her in one of the refugee camps. (After the war, many

NGO's – Non Government Organization - helped survivors find members of their families. In fact, one could hear public announcements on the radio, both in Europe and Israel, of survivors posting their names hoping to find live relatives). Not even one photograph of Lily survived the war and my hope was that perhaps the relatives in America, who fled before the war and took pictures of the family with them, would have one. That was not to be. Now only her faint memory is still with every fiber of my being. Her face was pale and angelic; she was a good hearted child and an excellent pupil, loved and adored by all, who died at the tender age of twelve.

Lily's death, I later realized, was just the beginning. It only started the process of the termination of the rest of my family. One morning, in the beginning of August 1943, I left the Ghetto as usual with our labor group toward the train depot. Our German supervisor walked on the street's sidewalk normally but we could sense heightened security traffic around us. To our surprise, we encountered small groups of fellow Jews returning to the Ghetto. They yelled at us in Yiddish, "Brothers, run away quickly. The Gestapo is capturing laborers and is taking them to train cars." The head of our group, Tuvia Sheres, gave an order to turn and walk back toward the Ghetto. Our German guard noticed the turn in direction, probably sensed that we were in danger and to our great fortune continued to walk without stopping us. We arrived back to the Ghetto's gate and safely got in. Once inside we heard that the German Army with the help of a militia group comprised of fighters from Lita, Latvia and Estonia, surrounded several predominantly Jewish labor camps, including Purobank Airfield and the train depot. They opened fire and started to shoot indiscriminately, killing and wounding many laborers. We feared for Dad, who was working at a saw mill with about 30 others in the vicinity of the provocation.

That evening he did not return from work as usual. I checked with the families of his co-workers and none had returned. We had no doubt that his group was captured or killed. Ghetto leaders tried to allay our fears and told us that the group was sent to another location in Estonia. A few dreadful days later, we received a letter from Dad through the Judenrat (the Jewish Administration). It simply stated that he was indeed in Estonia with a Jewish group and asked us to send him his tefillin (prayer phylacteries).

The wonderful news that Dad was safe in Estonia and was not sent to Ponar for execution was a big relief for Mom and me. But we were still very anxious about his fate and worried about his general health, which seemed to have deteriorated following the terrible loss of Lily at Bezadni. At that particular moment, the Ghetto experienced a decline in optimism and a deep malaise was shared by our community. The Germans and local leaders of the Ghetto tried, in vain, to reassure us that we were a vital resource for the war effort and therefore nothing bad would happen. Daily kidnapping and disappearance of thousands of our own shattered that empty promise and it became widely accepted that something big and tragic was awaiting us soon. In fact, our community began to talk about the final extermination of the entire Ghetto.

Soon thereafter, the Judenrat published an announcement whereby surviving kin of persons that were taken or kidnapped were to report to the authorities in order to be shipped to Estonia for "reunification." Very few people volunteered to register for the reunification, knowing full well the history of lies told by the Germans. Consequently, a decree was announced that everyone on the list published must report to the police station or risk arrest and death. When we looked at the list, mother's name was there but mine was not. I asked myself if it was a mistake or the work of my cousin Sonia Schemiavitz who was employed as a clerk by the Judenrat and omitted my name to save me. The police were brutal in enforcing this decree. Not only those refusing to register were punished, but they held the neighbors responsible for not turning in someone they knew were on the list. Mother decided that there was no alternative but to turn herself to the police. I objected vehemently to us separating, knowing that I would not see her again. Despite terrible danger, our neighbors agreed to keep mother at the apartment and I went to work the next morning as usual at the depot. When I approached the gate, there was a long line of laborers going through an extra careful security check. The Ghetto's police, along side the Germans, were checking each ID against the list of names for the expulsion. Those that were on the list attempting to exit the Ghetto were immediately taken to custody. When I returned later that day back into the Ghetto, I ran as fast as I could to our apartment on Shpitlana Street to look for mother. As I got close to the building I saw a policeman walking mother toward the police station. I begged him to let her go, alternating between arguing and crying, but to no avail. I could not separate from mother and decided to go with her to the police station. When we arrived, there was total chaos with hundreds of women and children crowded and panicked. I looked around, and at the right moment grabbed mother and ran with her outside unnoticed. We knew that we couldn't go back to our apartment and kept walking aimlessly in the narrowest Ghetto streets. We also knew that time was short as the night curfew quickly approached. Where could we go and who could we trust to take us in, risking their own lives? We remembered a widow friend of the family, Mrs. Esther Kaplan, who for years was a tenant in our building and was subletting a few units for income. I remember her charismatic son, Moshe Kaplan, was a unit captain in Vilna's "Beitar" chapter. (Beitar was a Zionist youth organization). We found her and I asked her to hide mother for a few days. She agreed without any hesitations and hid mother in a secret attic. I was overwhelmed with relief and joy to know that there was so much kindness against the constant brutality.

The hunt for family members who were ordered to be transported to Estonia for "unification" lasted four long days. A total of 4,000 people were purged from the Ghetto and, despite our fears, we found that they were not killed but shipped to labor camps in Estonia. I second guessed myself whether I made the right decision by preventing mother to go to Estonia to meet father. Prior experience made it clear to me that the Germans could not be trusted, while their ultimate goal was the complete annihilation of the Jewish population.

Mother returned to my apartment when things settled down, I continued to work at the train depot and she found a cleaning job with one of the Ghetto leaders. I remember those days as having better nutrition – as mother was able to bring leftover food from her job.

Another storm was brewing, however. The Germans arrested an underground communist activist, and, following brutal interrogation by the Gestapo, he revealed the name and location of the Jewish underground leader in Vilna. Yitzhak Vitenberg was the founder and commander of the fighting Ghetto's underground unit. (Yitzhak was revered by the community as a brave soul who espoused uprising against the Germans; his actions were not without controversy, as many – including the Ghetto's leadership – believed that cooperation with the occupiers would minimize the death toll). In the middle of the next night, units comprised of Germans, Lithuanians and a representative of the Ghetto's police entered his revealed hiding place and were attacked by his underground troops. They retreated and issued an ultimatum demanding his immediate surrender. Punishment for refusal was the complete burning of the Ghetto and its inhabitants.

The rebels, with their leader Vitenberg, encamped with all their weapons in an apartment house. They were guarded by the Ghetto's police, several groups of thugs and privileged labor groups who had close ties to the Ghetto's police chief Jacob Gens and marched to the beat of his drum. Vitenbers, dressed as a woman, escaped the building and found another hiding place elsewhere in the Ghetto. The community was torn between many, including the leadership, who asked for his surrender to save the lives of thousands. Others, in the minority, were willing to tie the fate of the entire community to the fate of the famed fighter – claiming that everyone would end up in Ponar's mass grave sooner or later and standing up to the enemy was the honorable thing to do. Even the underground group was divided between those wanting to escape to the forest and those who were inspired by the Warsaw underground who fought inside the Ghetto for years.

At the end, Vitenberg surrendered himself in order to save his people. He asked to speak to Mr. Gens, the Jewish police chief, and told him of his decision. According to one version of what happened next, the police chief offered Vitenberg cyanide to save him from the torture that surely awaited him in the SS building. In the pantheon of Jewish heroes, there should be no doubt that Yitzhak Vitenberg's name will be included.

A few days following the tragic death of Vitenberg, another decree was announced that the Ghettos would he shut hermetically. Thousands of us who were the privileged workers now wandered the streets aimlessly, adding to the general anxiety. Our hope for survival – based on the alleged need for skilled Jewish workers – evaporated now that we were not allowed to leave the Ghetto to report to work. We knew that the end of the Ghetto and its population was near, despite news of German defeat in Stalingrad by the Red Army.

Soon after, the Jewish chief of the Ghetto, Jacob Gens, was summoned to the Gestapo's office – a routine event. Except, this time he did not return. He was shot dead. The community mourned him and contemplated its own destiny. Mr. Gens was an officer in the Lithuanian army and was married to a local gentile woman. His wife and their daughter lived in a safe house outside the Ghetto. Because of his personal connections and relationships with the local officers, he could have easily saved himself, but instead he believed that he could navigate the community to become a productive contributor to the war effort and thus save lives. Historians will have to debate this tragic leader, weather he was a collaborator who gave us false hope, or a hero who saved many lives. There is no doubt, however, that at the end he was faced with an impossible situation he could not support and it cost him his life.

When we heard that the underground resistance groups escaped the Ghetto using the labyrinth of sewage pipes (they were assisted by a Jew who worked as a plumber for the city and had complete maps of the sewage system) and joined other fighters in the forest, we sunk into deep depression. We previously heard of arguments within the underground groups – whether to stay in the Ghetto and "protect" what was left of the community, knowing the fight had been already lost, or to escape and join the larger Partisan community where survival chances as well as a chance for real fighting were better with those arguing for the latter prevailed.

We were left hungry, tired and without leadership. What was left as a semblance of community now collapsed and we no longer had the energy to cope, knowing that the end of the Ghetto and those of us left in it was near.

▲ 347

347. לעבן דאָרף בוזורייסטיס.
דאָ האָבן די רוצחים זייערע קרבנות לעבעדיקע פֿארברענט אין
באראק פֿון טאָרף-קאריער, וווּ זיי האָבן געארבעט

347. על יד הכפר בוזוראיסטיס.
פה הרוצחים שרפו חיים את קורבנותיהם בצריף של המפעל
להפקת כבול שבו הם עבדו

347. Prie Buzuraisčio kaimo. Čia žudikai
savo aukas gyvas sudegino durpyno,
kuriame dirbo, barake

347. Near the village of Buzuraistis. They
were burned alive in the peat-bog barrack
where they worked

Memorial for the Bezadni's victims

Remnant of a barbed wire found at the Bezadni camp

Chapter 8

THE ANNIHILATION OF THE GHETTO

At day break on September 23, 1943, we saw many heavily armed troops made of Germans, Lithuanians, Latvians and Estonians donning full battle gear through our window. There was no doubt; the Ghetto's extermination had begun!

If we had to die, we would not do it hungry. Together with several hundreds of neighbors, I stormed an abandoned bakery and was able to put my hand on a loaf of bread but could not leave as the entrance was jammed with others trying to get in. Finally, after losing my shoes and suffering many bruises, I was able to get out. What a sweet victory – I had in my possession a full loaf of bread! I ran back to mom and the two of us with several others went into hiding in the lower level of the apartment at the back of a retail store. (Our building's main front was facing a major street outside the Ghetto that had shops at the street level). Each store had two entrances, front and back. The Germans blocked both sides with bricks but we were able to cut through the back side and had a few chairs, water and few first aid essentials. We closed the opening with a large armoire that had metal rings in the back. We pulled on the rings to bring the piece back and close the gap. We shared the hiding place with another family that had a two year old child. He was crying frequently, endangering all of us. Their grandmother said that she was willing to sacrifice herself with the child. To our great relief the child calmed himself and fell asleep.

We hid in the back of that store for six hours until the closet was moved from the outside and the Germans found us. They took us to the courtyard where we saw dozens of Ukraine guards. They were pushing and shoving us and hitting with the butts of their guns indiscriminately. One of the guards searched me and found my tefillin (phylacteries). After tossing it to the ground he raised his gun and, missing my head, hit my shoulder. As we were standing in the courtyard, other Jews that were discovered joined us. At the opposite side of the courtyard was a building that was used as an orphanage, housing about 50 children. Most of the staff abandoned them. The horrific cries of fear and hunger still ring in my ears to this day. We watched as all the children with the last two surviving caregivers were pushed into trucks and exited the Ghetto for extermination.

In the same way as most gates of that era were built, the gate at the entrance to the courtyard where we gathered was massive and was situated under a stone curved cover that created a portico on the inside. When fully open, a horse and buggy could get through it. The gates were open during the day and locked at night. They marched us toward the gate to exit the courtyard, and when we were just ahead of the gate, in the darkest part of the portico, I grabbed mom and shoved her and myself into the narrow space between the back side of the gate and the wall behind it. We stood still waiting to be discovered by the guards who were just few feet away on the other side of the massive door. I don't have a rational explanation for why we were not caught for hours standing there motionless. The time we waited for darkness felt like eternity. We heard constant movement of the Germans and their local Militia collaborators moving people out of the courtyard and the sound of hammer jacks breaking into hiding places. Once they found a hide out they would toss a grenade and we heard terrible cries of the injured as we stood clutching to each other waiting for darkness. Finally, at nightfall, all the guards left, and we went to the rear of the courtyard, found a staircase to sit and broke down crying.

We quickly had to find a place for the night fearing the return of the guards. I thought of another secret hide out in the building and I was hoping that it was not discovered. That particular place was similar to our other hide out except more sophisticated. The entrance was through an opening made by removing floor boards of the apartment above and using a makeshift ladder. The boards were then fastened back from the store on the bottom. We went up to the apartment found the spot were the opening was made and knocked several times but heard no reply. I whispered repeatedly into the cracks: "Jewish brothers and sisters don't be afraid we are your neighbors, Misha and his mother Chaya Schemiavitz. We are desperate for help." No reply! I then threatened to stay there until day break when the Germans would be back and all of us would be found. We then heard movement and they opened the boards for us and we joined a group of thirty five men, women and children. They had bunks built previously and had water and electricity. I saw a large sack of peas and in the center of the room a stove with a large pot cooking some peas. The smell of hot food made us dizzy as we haden't had any food or water in over 24 hours. In the corner of the store, they had a lavatory with a curtain for privacy. When we told them how we escaped from the guards by hiding behind the gate they could not believe us. We all realized that a miracle had happened. They apologized for not letting us in immediately because they feared that we were leading the guards to a hide out under duress. Their fears were not unfounded. There were many cases of Germans using Jews to find hide outs under threats of killing. There is no doubt that they took great risk by saving us.

I was amazed at how well this hide out was planned and how resourceful they were, having supplies, electricity and running water. They figured a way to connect to the water and the electric grid from the outside of the Ghetto. After a few days, the Lithuanians realized what was occurring and shut off the water and power. The occupants pulled out candles they stored and we started to use the limited amount of water stored in a barrel. When we were let in, they showed us a small cavernous area to be used if the hideout was discovered by the Germans. That small opening was covered by the sink and on its other side was an opening to the outside by moving few layers of bricks. At nights, some of us went out for fresh air and to search for food that was left at abandoned apartments. There was a strict ration of water favoring the elderly and the sick. Several of our people had very high fever, and one occupant, a Rabbi, lost his faculties and kept repeating Torah verses.

On the evening of Yom Kippur, October 9, 1943, my thoughts wandered to better days that seemed light years away. I thought back to reciting Kol Nidrei (all the vows and oaths we take) prayer at our synagogue during the evening service of Yom Kippur. The elders, including my grandfather, dressed in white garbs and large white yarmulkes as head covers. To me as a child, it seemed just like a scene from the Holy Temple in Jerusalem 2,000 years ago. The crowd would quiver as the Torah was taken out of the Holy Ark and the cantor encircled the Bimah, holding it against his chest and singing "Light is sown for the righteous, joy for the upright in heart." And during the Kol Nidrei prayer one could hear sobbing and begging from the women section. Even the men wiped a tear, and the children were too scared to make the slightest sound or motion as we were overtaken by the holiness and mystery of the moment.

In our dark and crowded hide-out, with very little time left, I thought about the Spanish Jewry during the Inquisition that – much like us – had to hide to recite their prayers during the high holidays. After all, Yom Kippur is the Judgment Day and according to the lithurgy of "Unetanei Tokeff" ("we acclaim this day's pure sanctity" – from the Musaf Service) our fate has been ordered by the Almighty between life and death. At that moment we all felt that indeed this Judgment Day would not bring life and our end was near.

We had not a drop of water to cook the few handfuls of lentils that were left and all of our efforts were focused on finding water. We were so desperate and dehydrated that a few suggested surrendering. "Listen Jews," said the Rabbi who we thought had lost his faculties, "I just dreamed that there is a barrel with water in one of the adjacent courtyards." Later that evening, with no alternatives, a few of us went to that courtyard and found several other Jews filling pots and containers with water that was intended for the laborers leaving the next morning. We drank a good amount and returned to our hide-out with a few buckets full, realizing that another small miracle had happened to us.

*   *   *

We whispered the Conclusion Service prayers of Yom Kippur "Pet-ach Lanu shaar" ("Open for us the gates even as they are clos-ing...") and meditated on how the notion of life and death was no longer abstract but very real. The next morning all was very quiet and calm when we heard foot steps, yelling and some shots being fired. It seemed that someone was discovered. At noon time there was more commotion and then knocks on our wall. The sink that covered the opening was removed and a strong beam from a flashlight was directed at us. We froze and I thought that we were found. Instead, to my surprise, I heard in Polish a demand from the intruders to pay in whatever valuables we had to keep our hide-out secret. We gave them few watches and necklaces in our posses-sion and as soon as they left I knew that they would not keep their promise. Shortly thereafter, several local police with SS officers entered our place and, using force and verbal abuse, took us out to the Ghetto's gate. I realized that due to carelessness the night before, we left a trail of water leading straight to our hide-out.

At the Ghetto's gate, we joined several dozen other Jews that were discovered in few of the last hiding places remaining, and together we were taken to the police station nearby. There, in a narrow courtyard, they shoved about eighty people, including my mother and I and the rest of those with whom we shared the hideout.

At the police station I heard two guards speak to each other in German. I had basic understanding of the language at the time and I understood that a German soldier was asking a Lithuanian officer what to do with all of us. This being a Sunday, there was no killing conducted in Ponar. Other officers joined the discussion of what to do with us until Monday morning when we would be taken to Ponar for execution. They ordered us to march toward the center of town on Zavalna Street.

It was a mild and beautiful early autumn evening, and the streets were full of local families strolling leisurely only to be distracted by the sight of us surrounded by guards.

The Lithuanian and Polish folks strolling by laughed at us and yelled anti-Semitic epitaphs. They could not have been more pleased. They took possession of the assets we left behind, invaded our homes and now watched us being taken away for good. We passed my school Tarbut where I studied since the first grade and where my sister Lily attended as well. My parents and the community attended many cultural events at the school auditorium. Many literary giants of the period visited the institution including Mr. Ossishkin, the famous poet H.N. Bialik and the beloved leader Dr. Jacob Vigoztki. From Zavalna Street we turned to Portova heading to the SS headquarters.

We entered the main courtyard of the building and walked down to the underground level that had prisoner cells on both sides. I noticed the infamous Gestapo executioner Keitel with several of his lieutenants. They separated the men from the women and children. He ordered every man to come before him. When my turn came he asked me how old I was and what my occupation was. I lied and said I was nineteen and was trained as a carpenter. He sent me off to join the group of men. All the women and children were pushed toward the end of the long corridor. Mother turned her head and waved goodbye to me. Together, with a group of about ten men I was pushed into a cell that already held about forty men. We had to lay on top of each other like sardines with no room to move and hardly any air to breath. At the corner of the cell was a single bucket overflowing with human waste. The stench was unbearable. The men told us that they had been in that cell for a week and could not understand why they were still alive. They too were some of the last survivors of the Ghetto in various hide outs that were discovered.

This was the first time that I was separated from my mother with whom I had a deep connection. The separation of eligible men from the women and children could only mean one thing – they would be taken to Ponar for execution. I could not stop crying all night thinking about my mother. In the morning the whole group was taken out to the bathroom and we were told that we had five minutes to use the facilities. There were four stalls and it was impossible for a group of over fifty men to accomplish this in five minutes. The guard beat us constantly with sticks and before I knew it we were back inside the cell with no relief for me. They threw a few loaves of bread at us and I was too upset and confused to eat, despite my hunger. Shortly afterwards, I became highly agitated and felt excruciating stomach pain and needed to go to the bathroom. I climbed and crawled over the other men towards the steel door and began to yell for help banging my fist on the door. My cell mates begged me to stop, fearing the guards' retaliation, but I was possessed and refused to defecate on top of other people. A guard came, opened the door and surprised me by letting me go to the bathroom. As I was led there, I saw a group of women returning from the bathroom and I saw my mother among them. She saw me and yelled in Yiddish: "Take care of yourself. You are young and have a chance to stay alive and live a full life." I yelled back:

"Mother, you are young too. They will send you to a work camp." That was the last time I ever saw my mother. The guard took me back to the cell without laying a finger on me, which shocked me and the other prisoners. I was overwhelmed with emotion from the unexpected and final meeting with my mother.

Early the same evening, as we waited for the guards to let us out to use the facilities again, the door opened and an SS officer holding a small note in his hand called my name to come outside. I froze and kept still. Another prisoner got up and said, "I am Michael Schemiavitz," and crawled towards the front. A few minutes later the imposter returned and again the officer called my name. This time I stood up identified myself and was taken out. I was asked to identify my former address and family information. Once he was satisfied that indeed it was me, I was told that under the orders of Mr. Kamenmacher, I was to join a maintenance facility of the Gestapo with a group of highly skilled Jewish laborers. I told the officer that I was not alone and that I would not go without my mother.

Kamenmacher was a wealthy and very resourceful Jew who was our neighbor and close family friend for many years. I remember my parents playing weekly card games with the Kamenmachers who also had a son my age. A very kind man, I'll never forget that at the time of my Bar-Mitzvah, although they were away on a skiing vacation, he left a beautiful watch as a gift for me. That watch became very special to me and I gave it to my father after he lost his watch at a labor camp just before I saw him for the last time. Mr. Kamenmacher fought for the German Army during WWI and received high honors for bravery. He used the Medal of Honor and connections to German brass to convince the Gestapo to let him create a highly specialized Jewish artisan group to help with the war effort. He succeeded in doing that as well as allowing the twenty four craftsmen to save their families as well. To be clear, this was not and should not be considered as collaboration with the Nazis. In fact, the whole group, including the Kamenmachers, was later executed by the Germans as they retreated from Lithuania days prior to the liberation by the Red Army. As a point of historic reference, I also want to note that many German Jews enlisted and fought dutifully for the German Army during WWI, a fact that explained the incredulity and disbelief by the German Jews that the Germans could hurt their own citizens during the rise of the Third Reich.

I returned to the cell and told the men what had happened, and they begged me to help them in joining the labor camp. On Monday morning, September 12, 1943, the last surviving Jews of Vilna did not get water, bread or permission to use the bathroom. We knew that this was ominous. We heard outside screams of women and children, guards yelling in German and Lithuanian and the sound of trucks. Then complete quiet. Shortly after, the door opened and a guard brought us bread and water. I was terrified about the fate of mother. Was she taken to Ponar already or perhaps they separated her and other healthy women for work? The door opened again and a guard ordered us to go outside and stand in groups of three. Twenty of the men were chosen and taken to a destination we did not know. As we were standing, the same Gestapo officer came and took me to another section of the prison. He opened a door and led me into a private cell with a window to the outside, a bed, a desk and a chair. "Stay here," he said, "Nothing bad will happen to you." "Where is my mother," I asked him, "She was here earlier. Please save her. Without her my life has no meaning." "We wanted to save her," he said, "But it was too late. When I came to take her, the group of women was already taken out to Ponar."

On the table I saw ten slices of bread and within them a note written in Yiddish that said: "I am sitting in this cell waiting for my execution. I will not touch this daily bread and the reader of this note will know how long I was here. My name is Biniakoski." (He was the Jewish head of the Ghetto for a short period after the execution of Mr. Genes). I laid on the bed and cried for my mother. I could not touch the bread of the dead man. In the evening the officer and Mr. Kamenmacher came into my cell. Kamenmacher set on the bed, hugged me and started to cry. He told me that on Yom Kippur he identified my mother and I in the group and did not stop his efforts to secure our release from the fated group. "Unfortunately," he said, "I could not save your mother who was a kind and gentle human being who always helped others in need."

Chapter 9

H.K.P LABOR CAMP

I was taken to a section of the SS headquarters where 20 to 30 Jewish artisans – the "Kamenmacher group" – worked at various shops. They enjoyed extraordinary privileges given in a time of war. They included tailors, shoemakers, jewelry smiths, graphic artists and fur experts and were granted unprecedented freedom of movement without having to wear the Star of David yellow tag that all Ghetto Jews had to wear. They were also allowed to have their immediate families with them. The fruits of their labor were for the benefit of top Gestapo and SS officers throughout Europe. They would receive furs, jewelry, suits and stacks of counterfeited English Sterling and Dollars crafted by these specialists. Immediately upon my arrival, I was treated with care and warmth. I was given a hot bath, new clothes, new shoes and a winter coat. The Jewish workers tried to cheer me up, but it was in vain. It was less than 24 hours since I lost my mother – the closest and most committed soul I had ever had. I could not stop crying and was oblivious to my surroundings. Two of the laborers escorted me on the train to the H.K.P (Hearst Kraft Park) camp where Jews with their families were staying. They were experts from a German Army maintenance unit that repaired tanks and other armored vehicles. The buildings stood in two rows and were built about a hundred years earlier by the Jewish community of Vilna in order to provide housing to the poor and were home to 1,200 Jews.

The Commander of the camp was a German Major by the name of Carl Plage` who treated the Jews with decency and fairness, a phenomenon that was unusual, given the prevailing anti-Semitic fervor of the period. When he became aware of the imminent termination of the Ghetto, he worked tirelessly to convince the SS leadership in charge of Vilna to save the lives of approximately 350 workers still living in the Ghetto who worked at various workshops. He made the argument that their expertise was essential for the war effort and offered to house them at H.K.P. When they refused to leave their surviving families behind, the authorities finally agreed to let them take their wives, parents and children – all totaling about 1,200.

Before the termination of the Ghetto, persons of authority at various workshops and maintenance facilities where Jews were employed attempted to convince decision makers in Berlin that those laborers were essential to the war effort and were indeed irreplaceable. These efforts were only partially successful. Following the termination, three pockets of Jewish laborers survived: the H.K.P (heavy armor maintenance facility), a garment shop dedicated to fur coats for the German Army (Kailis) and the "specialist" unit under Mr. Kamenmacher. These laborers had the privilege to be joined by their immediate families. At the Kailis camp, workers employed at the fur factory had lived with their families since the Germans entered Lithuania. As a result of this passport for life, literally, single men chose the most beautiful, young women to join as their fictitious wives, or commanded large fees from older wealthy women. There were rumors (which I can't confirm) that a few of the older men abandoned their older and sickly wives for younger attractive substitutes. My cousin Genya Schemiavitz who was an attractive young single, found a Polish widower who took her into H.K.P as his "wife." When the Gestapo brought me to the camp, I found her and joined her and her new "husband" and lived with them.

The Jewish supervisor of the camp, Mr. Kolish, knew of my arrival. He sent a policeman to summon me to his office and told me, "Be aware that under the protection of Mr. Kamenmacher you have special privileges. You will get plenty of food coupons and if you choose to work, let me know where you're interested in working." I told him that I would like to be employed and that I would work in the kitchen.

As I mentioned before, the two main buildings housed about 1,200 people – workers and their families, some included children and elder parents. Inside the camp complex were workshops for carpentry, metal works, sewing, upholstery, electric, shoe repair and a small factory for extraction of glucose from potatoes. The camp was guarded by German and Lithuanian and one permanent SS unit whose presence we did not feel with the exception of early morning line up. The heavy equipment repair shops were outside the camp proper and the mechanics employed there stayed for the week at a time and would return to our camp on Sundays. There was a mess hall for single men, but the families would normally eat in their apartments. I remember the mess hall to have a large "coffee" urn that was available twenty four hours a day. In the absence of real coffee beans, that beverage was made from wheat derivatives.

Once a week, Mr. Kamenmacher would come to pay a visit to Mr. Kolish. He would always visit me and bring me money and gifts. I befriended other teenagers, both male and female, and we would meet after work at one of the shops. I met and fell in love with a lovely girl named Rosa Bloch, whose father was employed at H.K.P. Young women who accompanied older men in order to save their lives befriended men their own age for company. As a young man of eighteen, I had many opportunities to meet attractive young women and to experience intimate relationships. The kitchen supervisor, Mr. Greener, was a clever and energetic Jew who was a fur merchant by profession. His wife was a team leader and the main cook. The German soldiers would bring deer and fox that they hunted in the forest nearby for Mr. Greener to clean and cut. To accommodate that activity, they arranged a shop in the basement and Mr. Greener took me as his apprentice. I spent many hours there, away from any watching eyes, toiling in light chores. In time, we'd added small farm animals such as rabbits, chicks and geese and even had a small pig that a soldier brought from a nearby farm.

With the addition of the small animals, I was now working day and night feeding the animals and cleaning up after them. Needless to say, I had absolutely no experience taking care of animals, and I was delighted to find a person at the camp who lived in a farm for years to assist me. Despite his help, we made mistakes that endangered us all. In one incident, a particularly mad German guard took interest in a pregnant rabbit and checked daily for the arrival of the babies – we were hoping to get few cigarettes from him for the special occasion. She delivered twelve, and before he came to check on them we found them all dead. I panicked and ran to notify Mr. Greener who was too scared to tell the bad news. Finally, the German arrived. When he saw the dead rabbits he was taken by rage, picked a wooden plank and started to hit us. I protected my head with my two hands and ran outside screaming covered with blood and bruises. We later found out that one is supposed to separate the babies from the adult rabbits after birth so that they are not chocked by them.

I scarcely recovered from this episode when another chapter occurred that almost cost me my life. My cousin Genya had a job with a young womens group at an army garrison outside H.K.P. One evening, she did not return to camp as usual. I asked her friends who returned where she was. I was told by one of them that she saw her after the shift change from her work clothes, tear off her Star of David yellow badge and leave the garrison with a German officer. Quickly, the rumor of her alleged involvement with the German, who helped her escape, spread throughout the camp. Her "husband" became suspicious that I knew of her whereabouts and threatened me to tell him, lest he would tell the Germans that I collaborated with my cousin. I begged and swore to him that I had no knowledge what-so-ever of her plan, but to no avail. He was enraged and humiliated and continued to threaten me. Finally, I decided to go to the Jewish leader of the camp and tell him about the threats. He called Genya's husband to his office, reprimanded him, and ordered him to leave me alone. A week later, I received a message through a Polish worker at the camp. Genya wrote that she was able to escape and was now with her sister Fanya who was hiding with her baby in the country (Fanya had a light complexion and blonde hair and could pass for a Polish woman). She vowed to help me escape the camp and join them at their hideout.

One morning I paid a visit to a classmate from Tarbut, Ychiel Sheres, who worked as a carpenter. The expression on his face

67

was ominous as he showed me what he was ordered to fabricate: a hanging structure. Like thunder, the rumor spread across the camp: who was the victim? Everyone feared for their lives. At noon, the entire camp was ordered outside under increased security, and we were told to stand at attention facing the hanging structure. In front stood the camp's German commander and next to him his Jewish counterpart. A car entered the gate and we quickly recognized the notorious murderer and liquidator of the Vilna's Ghetto and several other Jewish enclaves in Lithuania, the SS officer Keitel. With him sat a man we recognized from the camp with his wife and their five year old daughter. Keitel took them straight to the hanging site and with a wide smile told the crowd, "This will be the fate of those trying to escape this camp: death by hanging." He asked for five volunteers and not a person went forward. He then chose five men from the crowd and took the father to be hung first. He was tied and as they pulled the board from under his feet the rope broke. He fell to the ground. He crawled to Keitel's feet and begged for his life, knowing that it was not customary in Europe, even in wartime, to hang a person twice. His wife and daughter joined him in pleading for mercy. Keitel told the crowd cynically, "You Jews are looking for justice? Don't you know that you are sub-humans and therefore don't deserve protection from any laws?" He brandished his hand gun and shot the father and then the mother and the girl. We buried them at the corner of the camp, cleaned the pool of blood and said the Kaddish prayer for the dead. The experience of watching a family murdered in cold blood shook our collective souls deeply.

Another incident that raised our anxiety level followed shortly. A group of men, whose job was to cut wood for heating, left every morning to one of the nearby forests. On that particular day, they succeeded in contacting a group of Partisans in the forest and the leader, Tevke Sheres (Yechiel's brother) and few others escaped. Inside the camp, the guards immediately arrested Ychiel and their older father Mr. Sheres. They were held in the basement under guard and I had a chance to take them some food when I went down to feed the animals. When I left, we said goodbye knowing that their fate was sealed. None of us ever found who saved their lives, but the next day they were set free. A sliver of hope made its way to my heart – perhaps I would be able to escape and to join the Partisans as a fighter and avenger.

The relative calm we enjoyed at H.K.P. did not last long. Since my cousin Genya's escape, I lived in constant fear of being called in by the Gestapo and having to endure interrogations to find her whereabouts. I slept in the basement and kept low profile. Shortly after, the Germans announced that they planned to evacuate all the children and send them for "better care" elsewhere in order to provide a better environment for them and allow better productivity for their parents who would not have to care for their children. Fear and panic was shared by all the parents, knowing full well what the murderer's real intention was. Parents began to look for places and spaces to hide their children. Mr. Greener, our kitchen manager, had a three year old grandson and he had already made a plan. He arranged with a Polish family he knew that lived nearby to care for the baby. Every morning, a kitchen crew went to an apple grove just outside of camp's fence to fetch for water. On the arranged day, we carried the little boy inside a barrel and handed him to the awaiting Polish family. The Germans kidnapped dozens of kids during the event known as the "children action." I witnessed

69

scenes of separation – Germans grabbing crying children from their parent's arms – that will never leave my memory. In the archives of Jewish bravery and resistance, it is worth to name Mrs. Zukovsky, who spit straight at the face of a Gestapo officer that came to take her son. He shot her on the spot.

Following the "children action," the camp was in deep depression. The German commander of the camp, Major Plage, who was considered by us to be "father" of the Jews, tried to calm us saying that we still offered an essential contribution to the war effort and it was acknowledged by the authorities in Berlin.

At the turn of 1944, a dramatic turn of events occurred in the eastern front of the war. The Red Army was gaining ground against the Nazis and we felt a measure of hope that the Germans' end was near. But would we live to see victory day? Now more then ever, we felt the need to gather every ounce of energy and courage for the sole purpose of survival. The teenagers organized secretly for the purpose of escaping to the forest. Those with money hidden looked for hideouts among the country folk outside. Inside the camp we had plenty of supplies and craftsmen, and everybody joined in building secret hiding places underground and in attics. Fake walls were built in many apartments, and in the shops close to the fence, tunnels were dug. We were preparing for another "action" or the outright closure of the camp.

H.K.P camp with family and Israel's Chief Rabbi Goren, 1993

71

Chapter 10

LABOR CAMP KOZLOVA-RUDA

At the beginning of May 1944, the Germans notified the camp's commander that 50 men were needed to transfer to another work camp. The Jewish leadership compiled a list of men with no families who were eligible to work. The consensus among us was that being among the 50 was at best uncertain and at worse meant execution. I did not fear being included, as I was under the protection – or so I thought – of Mr. Kamenmacher. The guards gathered the 50 men in the building that housed the Jewish patrol. The kitchen staff was ordered to work a late shift to prepare food and beverages for the departure of the group early the next morning. As I was standing next to the large kettle preparing the fake coffee beverage, I added extra saccharine as a treat for the fated 50. I did not imagine that I would be enjoying that improved coffee the next day.

At midnight, a Jewish cop asked me to come with him to the police chief Tuvovine who was known from the Ghetto as corrupt and sadistic. When I came in, he told me to prepare to leave in the morning with the 50 men. I was very angry and told him that he would pay a price for kicking me out of the camp when Kamenmacher found out. He paid no attention to me and in the morning the group, myself included, climbed into military trucks that waited for us at the camp's gate. Within minutes, hundreds of the camp folks arrived to say goodbye, many of them crying and promising never to forget us. My girlfriend Rosa ran towards me, sobbing with a small package of goodies.

The trucks took us to the train depot guarded by German soldiers. The absence of SS and Gestapo officers relieved some of the fear we had. The train left the station and we knew that Ponar was only a few kilometers away. I waited anxiously to see if the train would slow down as we got closer to the site of the still active mass grave. It did not; the train kept going, but to what destination? We stopped at Kovno for a full day and we received supplies of bread and water. At dawn, we were ordered to get out of the cars for a change of guard. To our dismay, a Lithuanian militia took over – often the local militias had to prove their brutality over that of the Germans. The Lithuanians called us to order and we crossed the railroad lines to a waiting cargo train that seemed to be fitted for short distance travel. It was a cold and rainy day and I remember thick forest on both sides of the train as we rode exposed to the elements. The cars were open – designed for bulk transport, and we sat in puddles of water, shivering from the cold. After a while, the train stopped in an open field. The guards went out, gathered several fallen tree limbs, sat, took out few bottles of vodka and food and enjoyed a relaxing picnic. After they had enough to drink and became visibly inebriated, they set up the empty bottles as targets and started to shoot at them. When they were done with the bottles, they picked a few men from the train and sprayed shots over their heads. Luckily no one got hurt. Shortly after, the "picnic" was over and we continued onward.

Our destination was a fenced camp with barracks and four guard towers. We entered through the main gate and the Lithuanian guards left us with what seemed to be an older German Army reserve troop. Each barrack was relatively comfortable with wooden triple bunks, wool blankets and a heater. A Jewish supervisor greeted us and gave us warm soup and bread. He was a decent and warm young man from Kovno and he told us that the camp had approximately 350 men and women. He said that everyone would be working in the peat digging operation under the supervision of German authority (peat was used as a source of energy among other things). The guards were older soldiers and the leadership was made of officers that were wounded lightly on the front lines. With the exception of punishment for poor productivity and insubordination, the treatment would be reasonably good and free of physical abuse he told us.

The peatland mine was operating 24 hours a day and every week we switched the shift. The labor was extremely hard without a moments rest. The wet and muddy peat was extracted by a huge bulldozer. Our job was to load the wet peat unto wooden planks with shovels and then to transfer it in blocks weighing 40 kilos (88 pounds) to a drying field a few hundred meters away. During our eight hour shift, we received no breaks. Most of the women were assigned to cleaning or cooking chores, but a few of the stronger, young women worked with us in the mine.

The camp was about 40 kilometers from Kovno and was called by the Lithuanians "Kaslo-Ruda" but was known to us as "Kozlova-Ruda." The mature German guards did not interfere with the daily routine of the camp so long as it was productive. They entrusted a Jewish doctor from Kovno to run it. He had one Jewish guard to help him, and I regret terribly that I can't remember the names of the two gentlemen who were kind and humble human beings. The Jewish guard would wake us to get ready for our shift, saying in a warm and fatherly voice "Kinderlaech (children in Yiddish), please wake up, it's time to go to work. You know that if you're late, you and I will be punished." He was our addressee for all of our questions and disputes, and we looked to him as our trusted friend. We had enough to eat, having a diet of one slice of bread and soup per day. From the nearby Ghetto in Kovno, we received additional loaves of bread and, for a while, had two slices per day.

The relatively lax security at the camp and the proximity to a large regional city and many farms produced an active black market of product exchange without interference by the German guards. Farmers brought potatoes and bread in exchange for clothing items we had in the camp. Those among us who had certain skills would repair shoes and sew clothes for the farmers in return for products. There was also a talented tailor and he was busy making and repairing clothes for the German guards. A highly ranked officer asked him to make a pair of riding breaches for him. When he tried the new pair on in front of his comrades they ridiculed him because they were too wide and he looked like a swan with its wings spread. His feelings hurt; he ran to the tailor's barrack, ordered him out and threatened to kill him. Our leader finally convinced the officer that a fine pair would be made by the finest tailors in Kovno and the episode culminated in the beating of the tailor.

Not all was calm, as we experienced periodic spasms of violence and fear. During one incident, an officer was missing pieces of his wardrobe, which we stole as a means to barter for various items. He ordered everyone to stand outside at attention and threatened that unless the perpetrators came forth, he would start executing prisoners. We stood for hours, fearing the worst, but our leader, again, with his cleverness convinced him to order us to work Sunday as a collective punishment.

From the area's farmers, we learned that there were many bands of Partisans in the nearby forest, who, in the dark of night, confiscated food, clothing and even horses from them. This news encouraged us tremendously, and we decided that it was time to attempt an escape to the woods. Our barrack was approximately 15 meters from the fence, and we started to dig a tunnel at night, after pulling up a few of the floor boards. We had no problems getting the shovels needed from our friends working at the equipment warehouse. We devised a plan that included shifts of digging, improvised trusses to support the weight and a way to get the soil out. That was simply done by stuffing our pockets and emptying them inside the outhouses. The plan was moving at a rapid pace, and after two weeks we dug three to four meters.

One night in June we heard machine guns and explosives. We hoped that it was the Partisans attacking the camp's guards. In the morning, the guards ordered us to go to work as normal. Later that day we heard from the Lithuanian workers that indeed it was the Partisans who destroyed a section of the railroad used by the Germans for supply trains and telephone poles. They attacked these targets that were guarded by Lithuanian police. That day, our German guards were visibly nervous and held their guns with a sense of urgency. Inside our camp, security tightened and flood lights were added to the guard towers. The Germans ordered us to dig defense trenches around the barracks and pour concrete shelters for machine guns. Despite the fact that we had to work harder now, at heart we were pleased to see that the Germans were

showing signs of fright. There was no doubt from the news we
gathered that the German Army was in retreat and the end of this
war was near. But would we live to see victory day? We continued to
spend sleepless nights digging the tunnel – a few more meters to
the fence and additional ten to the other side of the fence at the
edge of the forest!

The beginning of July 1944 brought with it torrential rain that
lasted for days. We were wet and cold to the bone working the
open peat pits, knee deep in mud, wearing wooden shoes that hurt
our feet and caused many blisters. Despite the cold temperatures,
we were sweating and feeling the exhaustion of the hard labor.
The guards covered themselves with wool blankets as we counted
the hours to the end of our shift when we'd get back to our barracks to dry off and rest by the stove. When we finally arrived back
at the camp, German and Lithuanian guards waited for us and
instructed the group to follow them. They marched us for a few
kilometers in a muddy pathway in the rain that would not stop.
We arrived at a small improvised bridge and noticed that a military lorry caused it to collapse, blocking a long German convoy
from crossing. We joined another group of Jewish prisoners from
our camp in an attempt to dislodge the vehicle, but it would not
budge. A group of German soldiers now joined the effort, and
they, too, could not make a difference. The Germans decided to
abandon the truck and their convoy for the time being and return
with us to the camp. When we arrived back, tension was palpable
and we saw that the camp was surrounded by hundreds of guards.
In the center court stood all the prisoners, men and women, the
leader of the camp, the German commander and his lieutenants.
I had no doubt that the Germans were ordering the elimination

of the camp. The tunnel was incomplete and therefore useless for a quick escape. This was clear – the evacuation of the camp was certain. During the subsequent nights we heard constant gun fire of what we thought was the retreating Wehrmacht. Indeed we confirmed with local farmers of the rapid advance of the Red Army and the panicked retreat of the Germans.

The hour of salvation was near! Would I survive the very last period of horror after years of suffering? Was it possible that the Germans, while in retreat from the Russians, would continue with the extermination of Jews? I could not fathom that they would have the resources and determination to send trucks at that hour to pick up the remaining 400 Jews in the middle of the forest for slaughter.

One morning they led us to a country road away from the camp and we all marched very slowly in deep mud, pondering our destination. At dusk, a thick fog descended onto the forest and visibility was minimal. All of a sudden we heard "Hurrah, Hurrah" – the Russian battle cry. Our guards fell to the ground pointing their guns at the source of the cries.

I jumped over the head of the guard next to me and began to run toward the trees as if I was struck with lightening. Bullets were whistling all around me but I kept running at full speed, sweating heavily and then feeling heat on my back. I threw my backpack and saw that it was on fire. I continued to run for about an hour until I collapsed from total exhaustion. Around me was total silence: no Germans, no guns, only me and the trees. I was free! I was free! What an incredible feeling. I remember thinking that it did not matter what might happen next, I finally tasted freedom and it was all I wanted and hoped for.

As I was resting, thinking about what to do in the morning, I head footsteps. I feared Germans or local militia who were notorious in cooperating with the Nazis and gladly murdered many of our people. I also thought of the wild boars that inhabited the forest and were quite dangerous. I wanted to get up and run but I froze with fear. I then saw a Jewish prisoner from my camp who escaped at the same time I did. We hugged and kissed each other with great joy and relief that we were not alone. Together we would somehow manage. We stayed in the forest that night and the following day, drinking rain water and eating wild berries that were in abundance.

Chapter 11

THE ESCAPE TO FREEDOM

As the sun was setting on the next day, we started our way out of the forest in search of food and safety. After a long walk, we saw a wheat field at the edge of a small hamlet. Hiding in the distance, we observed for a while and saw children playing, which implied to us that the population of the village was relatively young and, most likely, not sympathetic. We decided to turn back and search for another village which we found after walking some kilometers. We were very tired and suffered from a keen sense of hunger by the time we noticed dim lights at a distance and heard dogs bark faintly. As we got closer, we saw that several farmers went outside searching for the cause of the commotion. In desperation, we took great risk and approached one farmer. With broken Lithuanian we told him that we escaped the work camp and all we wanted was food, as we haden't had anything to eat in two days. Frightened and agitated, he told us that he would leave us some bread at the gate, and asked us to depart immediately because his life was in danger should the Germans find that he helped Jews. To our question of what the distance was from the village to the camp, he said that following the tracks, it was 20 kilometers. He added that our life was in danger because military and police units, in retreat from the Russian Army, were all around us. We ate the bread he left us, found some clear spring water and fell asleep outside the village until the sun woke us the next morning.

We knew that local collaborators, police and militia, used the villagers for shelter and food, and therefore it was just too risky to approach another hamlet. We became very concerned about our prospects of finding food and with no real alternatives, began the journey back to the camp. We were hoping to find it abandoned in order to find food, clothes and blankets. Early the next morning, we arrived at the camp's fence; we squatted at a distance for observation. We could not believe our eyes! Dozens of prisoners, including women were at the courtyard with several armed guards. We noticed that the guard towers were not staffed and gathered that they all returned to the camp. To our further surprise, the main gate was not guarded and folks came in and out as they pleased. We approached the gate and I immediately recognized several friends from H.K.P. in Vilna. Apparently, about 150 men escaped into the woods at the same time I did, including three armed guards, a Russian and two Uzbeks (the Germans recruited POW's to help with guarding prisons and work camps).

The Russian, an officer in the Red Army, gathered everyone in the center of the yard. He spoke in Russian and said that he was forced to become a guard by the Germans after his capture, and that his loyalties lie with the Red Army, which was approaching closer every day. He further mentioned that he trusted that we would vouch for his fair treatment of all prisoners. He then proposed a plan of action which was to split into groups of ten and fan into the woods to wait out the remaining days until the Russians arrived. Unfortunately, the food supply that I was hoping to find in the camp was emptied by those who arrived before me. However, I was able to find a sheep's skin coat to stay warm. I joined a group of 12 made up of friends and acquaintances from Vilna, including two married couples. We followed the officer's instructions and started to march toward the woods with no specific destination.

After a walk of a few kilometers, we found a thicket of vegetation and decided to hide there for the time being. After a rest of a few hours, a group of several men were sent to look for water and food. Specifically, they looked for potato fields, hoping to pick and bring back ripe ones for us to eat. Before their return, a farmer, herding a few cows, discovered us and quickly ran away. When our friends returned, we decided to move to another location, fearing the farmer would notify the local police. We wandered many more kilometers looking for a suitable place to survive a few more days. We decided to move every two days. One day we encountered three armed men. First we thought surely they were Partisans and we showed open excitement and adoration. We asked for their help in joining the Partisan encampment, but they responded by asking us if we had any weapons. We knew that on the one hand, we were useless to the Partisans without weapons, and on the other, if we told them that we did, they might harm us and take them. Their behavior was suspicious and I thought that they might be just criminals. We told them that if they would allow us to join, we would bring our weapons (which, of course, we didn't have) that we hid in one of the camp's barracks. We agreed to rendezvous the following night but the group decided not to trust them and flee.

Hunger, sleeplessness, bugs and endless rain took a toll on the group. Some of us sank to a hapless depression and stopped functioning while others started to argue and even fight. Most trouble came from a couple of unscrupulous men who made matters worse. Two disturbing incidents I remember well. First, they suspected that one of the married couples had hidden jewelry and one day used force to search their clothes. The rest of us stood together to their defense and they backed off. The second incident involved my cherished coat that provided me with warmth and protected me from the rain. One of the guys decided that he wanted the coat accused me of stealing it from him and, once again, the group stood up and he backed off. Secretly, the rest of us consulted and we contemplated a way to leave the men but eventually we realized that they were quite resourceful and useful in stealing food from farmers and decided to stay together.

Artillery noise in the distance became nearer and louder by the day. Over us, we saw low flying fighter planes with the red star insignia of the Russian Army. From nearby roads we heard the roar of heavy trucks and tanks. We got deeper into the forest, expecting German soldiers fleeing for shelter into the woods as well. At one instance, we scouted a German unit carrying guns and their officer on horse back. It was apparent from their hasty pace that they were in retreat. I had no doubt – the end of the war was near. I remember thinking that, now more then ever, as I was so close to the end of the nightmare, it was critical to stay strong, not to take too many risks in looking for food inside or close to villages and to let events unfold patiently. The noise from the roads of army moving subsided and the Russian fighter planes gave room to high altitude bombers. Then it was eerily quiet, and the following twenty four hours were wrought with anxiety and readiness. In the morning, we heard the sound of a tank battalion – were the Germans fighting back? Then quiet again and we heard the chatter of soldiers. We suspected that a unit was resting in a nearby road. One of us volunteered to get closer and listen to their language. He came back shortly and told us that he couldn't get close enough to ascertain the tongue they spoke without being sighted. Among us, was a handsome blond young man who could easily pass as a local. He was also fierce and creative and he offered to check things out. After a short hour, we heard him scream in Yiddish as he returned "dahs iz die roitee armee, meer zeiney freiy, meer zeiney freiy."

The words he spoke still reverberate in my head: "It is the Red Army, we are free, we are free."

We ran as fast as we could toward the road and met a supply platoon of the Red Army. We hugged and kissed the surprised soldiers who were "attacked" by ragged and emaciated prisoners with hallowed look. This was an encounter between tough Russian fighters who fought a bloody war with the Nazis and the first Jewish survivors they saw. The years of suffering and starvation were stamped all over our bodies and faces and we could see our reflections in their eyes. Their commander, riding on a horseback, asked who we were and where were we from. We told him we were Jews who escaped the German occupation. He came down from the horse and said, to my shock, in Yiddish: "Eer ziet dach mienie breeder." – "You are my brothers!" He then told us that he was a Jew and wanted to know how we managed to survive. He said that he marched with the Red Army thousands of kilometers and witnessed destruction and murder of our people, including his own family. You are still in danger, he said. The front is too close for your safety and you must continue to hide. He then ordered a supply truck to take us to their encampment about 20 kilometers to the east. In a hidden area surrounded by woods, we came upon a temporary base and saw ammunition, food and other supplies. The commanding officer ordered the cooks to make a thick soup with bread for us. After we were fed he told us that they expect to be bombarded by the Germans and we should leave for our own safety.

The group started to walk toward Kovno, alongside a road with heavy traffic of Red Army equipment. We showered the soldiers with thanks and blessed the Red Army, the Soviet Union and even Comrade Stalin. That evening, we stopped at a Lithuanian village and chose a large, comfortable house to settle in for the night. We ordered the housewife to feed us and make arrangements for sleeping. She told us firmly that she would provide us with food, but the rooms are reserved for Russian officers that she expected. We responded angrily and told her that if she objected, we would kick her out of the house and take over ourselves. One of her daughters ran outside to find Russian soldiers to help her mother. Minutes later, a few Russians came in and asked whether it was true that we entered that house without permission. We told them that it was our right to demand accommodations from the locals who collaborated with the Germans. The administration of justice was up to the authorities, not for civilians, we were told, and if we didn't leave, they would arrest us and bring us to a military trial. We were completely shocked! The Red Army was protecting the rights of murderers while threatening us, who had been the victims for years. That episode was the first reminder – which I later found to be all too typical – that the Russians authorities would afford us no sympathy and little consideration or privileges. On the contrary, the Soviets treated the survivors with suspicion. This cynical attitude included the treatment of Jews and even Red Army POWs. If one survived, it must have meant that they collaborated. Days, nights, months and years we struggled to merely survive and now that the day we waited for had arrived, with no immediate danger to our lives, we faced suspicion and antipathy. I remember thinking about our situation, we lost our homes, our families had been murdered, and as we walked for days aimlessly through pastoral villages looking for temporary shelter, we had to listen to children's playful voices and farmers working their fields completely oblivious to our situation and the raging war.

Onward we walked, lonely, depressed, and covered with fleas, human remnants of a Great People that once was and is now gone.

We finally arrived at the city of Kovno. Our first encounter at the outskirt of town was with a group of gypsies that came out of hiding in the woods. We regarded them with sympathy as they too – as a people – were sentenced to death by the Nazi ideology. After hugs and kisses of those who understood what it meant be brutalized and to survive, we advanced together toward the center of the city, searching for the office of the commander in charge of Kovno. On our way, we ran into a group of survivors from the Kovno Ghetto who directed us towards two centers that were hastily created for Jewish refugees. One was located in the Red Cross building and the other in a prenatal clinic on a main street. We turned to the clinic and were welcomed warmly and given rooms to rest with beds, sheets, pillows and blankets. Such luxury I had not enjoyed in years. They let us bathe with warm water but had no new clothes for the group so we had to get into our dirty, flea filled garments. We pulled the mattresses to the floor trying to avoid soiling the rooms of the clinic. As we ate a wonderful warm soup, we heard emergency sirens and then the announcement that city was bombarded by the Luftwaffe. Everyone but us went down to the basement. After we ate we went to sleep on the clean mattresses.

In the morning we met a group of Jewish Partisans who survived in the forest as an improvised militia. They took us to the city's military governor where we met a few hundred other Jewish survivors, a few of whom gathered at Kozlova-Ruda camp after its abandonment. With them were also the three guards that escaped with us. Most of them were given shelter at the Red Cross center. The previous night during the bombardment, the Red Cross building received a direct hit and four of the Jewish refugees were killed. We were in shock, realizing that four of our brothers who survived years of horror, perished only hours after reaching freedom.

In total, about 160 of us escaped Kozlova-Ruda and only 95 made it to Kovno. We suspected that the rest did not make it to liberation. We found that some fell into unfriendly ambush (probably Lithuanian militia). Others met the retreating German Army, and a few were murdered by farmers when they asked for food. At the military headquarters we were debriefed and given official papers. During the debriefing, we gave friendly testimony regarding the three Russian guards who escaped with us. Later, as we stood outside, I noticed a handsome, tall fellow I didn't recognize, who seemed a good natured and determined person. We started to talk and I found that he wanted to return to Vilna. That, of course, was my desire as well – to go back home – and we decided to make the voyage together. After obtaining passage documents we headed towards the road leading to Vilna. A large crowd had already gathered at the intersection of the road to Vilna and soldiers searched everyone carefully. In small groups, they took us to the officer in charge, who had the rank of major in the Red Army and had worn his medals. When he found out that I was Jewish, he introduced himself as Jewish as well. He said that their mission was now to capture the local collaborators with the Nazis and they needed our help. He asked me to gather a group of survivors, and shortly after, I brought back to him a small group of men and women. He separated the group between those who were fluent in Lithuanian and those of us from Vilna who spoke it just a little. He asked those fluent to help with interrogating suspects and released the rest of us after arranging a military truck to take us to Vilna.

As the truck got close to the outskirts of my city, my heart was pounding with anticipation and trepidation. I kept a sliver of hope that I might find my father and sister alive as I did not witness their death. They dropped us at a military base outside the city and we had to walk to the center of town several kilometers heading towards Third and May Street where I lived until we were corralled into the Ghetto. My companion, Asher Isaac told me on the way that his family was from around the town of Turgel, not far from Vilna, where they owned and worked the land for many years and that he naturally knows many of the locals there. He suggested that we should make the trip there because he was confident that we would have all our needs met by his neighbors. (It was uncommon but not unheard of for Jews to be land owners in Lithuania, especially dating back to the Polish rule). We decided to stay the night in Vilna and leave for Turgel the next day. We arrived at my house as night was falling. The first thing I noticed was that the corner of the house, where our apartment was located, sustained a direct hit by a bomb but was not destroyed. As we got closer we saw that the blinds were drawn shut and the gate to the courtyard was locked.

We made our way to my uncle Yrmiyahou's apartment – which was partially hit – on the second floor through an opening to the stair-well. We entered the apartment. Almost immediately we collapsed on the floor and slept the night completely exhausted. As the sun came up, I opened my eyes and looked at the ceiling which had partially collapsed in the room that was my uncle's bed room. I loved going to his apartment because it was beautifully decorated and he had an artist paint all the ceilings with different motifs. In his own bed room, the artist painted a celestial panorama of starts and four moons, one in each corner. As I was lying there, the stars and the moon flickered at me, reminding me of the sweet souls of the family I lost. These stars were the first memorial candles I began to observe for the rest of my life.

Chapter 12

THE RETURN TO VILNA

In the morning Isaac and I headed on foot, as we planned, towards the end of town, where the roads led to his village's direction. We hoped to catch a ride with a military truck or a farmer with a carriage – but neither materialized. We walked a distance of 30 kilometers to the village of Turgel. It was a hot August day and my feet swelled and developed many blisters that bled with each step. I wore heavy rubber boots that were designed to work in the muddy open peat pits which I found upon my return to the work camp. I hardly took them off my feet for weeks and the pain became so unbearable that I just couldn't walk any longer. I sat at the side of the road and I told Asher Isaac to continue without me. He said that he would not leave me and began to waive frantically at the vehicles passing on the road. He was successful in stopping a farmer leading a horse that was pulling a carriage full with his field's harvest. There was room only for one of us and he sat me next to the farmer and walked alongside as we headed to Turgel.

We arrived at his village at dusk and immediately saw a group of armed men at the entrance wearing civilian clothes and donning a red arm band. There was no end to our happiness when we found that they were mostly Jews who survived with the Partisans and were now patrolling the vicinity in the absence of law and order. One of them led us to a communal location that housed dozens of Jews that survived either in the surrounding forests or hiding in barns and other structures in one of the hamlets. Isaac was anxious to return to his own farm to find the farmers that worked his family's fields. The rumor of Isaac's return preceded our arrival to the farm. Dozens of men and women went out of their homes cheering us as we approached. An argument ensued as to who would have the honor to host Isaac and his friend. It was settled that one wealthy farmer would host us and many others. We had a feast with huge amount of food and lots of vodka. The locals were telling stories of sacrifice and endangerment to protect and hide their Jewish neighbors. They continued with tales of suffering during the war when their crops were taken by the German Army or stolen by Partisans. Isaac, who had copious amount of vodka, listened intensely when all of a sudden, to my astonishment, he got up and started to yell and cuss in Russian at our hosts. His face was red and flames shot out of his eyes as he said, "How dare you complain about your suffering. You helped the Germans and Lithuanians in eliminating your Jewish neighbors so you could steal their property. It's time to avenge this injustice and for the killers and collaborators to pay the price. We shall not stay here another moment in the presence of traitors, but we will return and you will feel the full extent of Asher Isaac's revenge".

As we left the farm heading back to Turgel, we heard shots being fired from the direction of the forest. A local we spotted close by told us that the source of the shooting was an underground Polish unit known as A. K (Armia Kriyova), that the exiled Polish government in London organized and financed. The purpose of these units was to attempt some control over the occupied Polish land by both Russian and German forces. The A.K. units were known anti-Semites who killed hundreds if not thousands of Jews who ran to the woodlands seeking a hiding place.

We arrived at the house where the Jews were concentrated. A few soldiers advised us to fan out into local homes because of a fear that the Polish underground may strike against us that night. We found shelter in one of the barns at the village. All night we heard shots exchanged between the Poles and the Russian Army. In the morning I quickly decided that it was too tenuous a situation and told Asher Isaac that I was going back to Vilna. He wanted to stay. We said our goodbyes and I caught a ride with a Russian truck back to Vilna. I never saw him again nor ever knew what happened to him. My plan now was to go back to our house, seek some of our older neighbors and ask for shelter.

I first went to the apartment of a Polish officer at the street level, next door to the butcher shop. He and his family received me very warmly and seemed to be happy that I survived. They welcomed me to stay with them, but I refused because I was still covered with lice. Before dinner time, other neighbors arrived to greet me, including one person I didn't recognized. He was a carpenter that performed odd repair jobs at the building. He told me that during the winter months he and his family were hungry for food and only my father would pay him in advance toward future repairs at the building so they would survive. Then he said, "I feel a moral obligation to help you because of the deeds of your father. My wife and daughter are in the country picking potatoes and until they return you'll stay with me." I told him that I had lice and he said not to worry, he would help me. When we got to his apartment, he filled several large pots with water to boil, sat me in a large tub and started to scrub my entire body with chunks of hardwood and hot water. He burned all my clothes in the furnace and gave me some of his garments that were several sizes too large for me. I will never forget the kindness that that person, Nicolas Koozi, showed towards me with his warmth and caregiving.

In the morning, I peeked outside the window and discovered that I was looking straight at the windows of our apartment across the courtyard. I imagined that I was seeing my family moving about, my mother, father, my sister and grandmother. I stood there and started to cry uncontrollably. Nicolas came into my room, saw me cry, hugged me and asked what the matter was. I told him that as long as I stayed at his apartment I would not stop looking at our windows across. After few days of gathering the emotional strength needed, I decided to go to my apartment. I found several families that evacuated their damaged apartments during the heavy fighting as the Russian Army entered the city. I found in my apartment some of our family's furniture including a beautifully made china cabinet, an oak writing table and other pieces as well. I asked the inhabitants to vouch in writing that the furniture belonged to me and to keep it until I was able to fetch it. I went into the attic to look for specific framed photographs that I remembered – those of my grandparents, my parents wedding picture and other family pictures that I hid the day of our expulsion into the Ghetto. To my great sorrow, I could not find them.

I then went to visit Dr. Kasperoweitz. I remembered him and his wife as very good friends of my parents. During the Polish regime, Dr. Kasperoweitz was the head of the health department of the city. He was a noble man, a liberal who was furious at his fellow Poles who showed any signs of anti-Semitism. I sat with him and his wife for many hours detailing the demise of my family, my community and my journey to survival. Since that visit, his wife would bring a hot meal to me which I shared with Nicolas who was poor. He was not ashamed of his poverty. In fact, he was proud of being poor, as it was evidence that he didn't take anything from his Jewish neighbors.

At the end of the week Nicolas' wife and daughter returned from the country and were not pleased to find that there was a guest in the house. Nicolas asked me to stay in my room and I could hear his wife yelling and demanding her husband to throw me out. I knew that Nicolas was torn and would never ask me to leave so I decided to save him from this unpleasant predicament and told him that I would like to move on. I packed my few possessions and as I left the apartment I had absolutely no idea where to go. I hardly left the center courtyard of the building when I heard Nicolas calling my name. Come back, he said, my wife has relaxed and agreed for you to stay with us. I returned to the apartment and shook Nicolas' wife's hand warmly and told them that I would never forget their goodness and would do all I could to repay the favor.

The next day, I went out to look for Jewish survivors who, like me, might have returned to the city. I made my way to the main Vilna synagogue. In the courtyard in front of the Temple I met Jews who survived in the woodlands with the Partisans, some who found hiding places in the country and others, like myself, who survived forced labor camps. A few of them found odd jobs and from their clothes and general disposition, it seemed that they had decent nutrition. I had a very emotional chance reunion with two school friends from Tarbut, Elijah Svirski and Abraham Karpinkes (who later, in Israel, changed his last name to Keren Paz) – both of whom have since passed away. They told me that a third friend with whom they spent the war years, Vilkomirski, was killed close to the end by the Germans. Through one of the survivor's contacts I found a job at a leather processing factory. The Germans left a large amount of coal and potatoes outside of the plant and my job was to keep a log of the transfers of these goods by the Russian Army to various locations. I quickly discovered that many shipments never made it to the assigned destination, but rather, found their way to the black market, with no real objection or oversight by the Russians. I arranged a load of coal and potatoes to be delivered to Nicolas's apartment. They could not believe how quickly I repaid the favor.

A rumor began to circulate that a large gathering of the survivors would take place at the central Temple for the coming Yom Kippur prayers. The events and emotions of that night will stay with me forever. When I arrived to the large yard in front of the Synagogue, I saw hundreds of Jewish Red Army soldiers and officers, men and women. Inside, there was no room to stand, and many wore Russian uniforms. As the prayer began, there was a collective cry akin to a howling that started from the section of the small group of survivors and spread like a wild fire to the entire congregation, including the soldiers – Jews and non-Jews alike. It is worth noting that it became apparent to the Jewish worshipers that at least half, if not more of the people in the temple, were not Jewish, but neighbors and soldiers who felt the personal need to partake in that solemn day.

The Temple stood for hundreds of years and became the focal point for generations of Jews in Vilna. It was used during the German occupation as a food supply distribution center and was completely destroyed by the Russian authorities in 1949 under mysterious circumstances. The greatest cantors started their careers at our Temple, and with the blessings of Vilna's selective congregation, made their way to the rest of the world's stage. I used to go there with my father to hear the choir sing with the cantors to the great delight of the community. I was fortunate to hear the singing of such venerable cantors as Gershon Syrota, Moshe Kosovitzki, Schteinberg and the last great cantor prior to the calamity, Eidleman.

Following the liberation a typhus epidemic spread throughout the city and surrounding area. The Soviet Union was still fighting the Germans in the Western front and the Red Army had many installations in the area with heavy traffic of personnel and equipment. The army's medical leadership was keen on containing the epidemic lest it would spread to the fighting army in the west. To that end, they sanitized many parts of the city and posted warnings and instructions about how to keep the population clean. They ordered the citizenry to turn in anyone that was sick in bed and I was concerned about Nicolas who was running extremely high fever and lay helplessly in bed. He begged me not to notify the authorities afraid that he would be quarantined.

The next day I followed him with high fever and could not move my legs, let alone get out of bed. Mrs. Kasperoweitz knocked at my door but I couldn't get up to let her in, I tried with all my might to speak loud enough for her to hear me and luckily she heard me call her name. She summoned a medical crew; they broke the door and quickly took both Nicolas and myself to the quarantine barracks outside of town. Dozens of soldiers lay in beds cramped next to each other, with doctors and nurses scurrying about trying to help. Nurses took turns putting wet towels with cold water on my forehead in an attempt to reduce the temperature. A Catholic priest came by to encourage and pray with the soldiers. When he came to my bed and offered the cross for me to kiss, I whispered through a delirious state of mind that I was Jewish. He sat next to me and asked if I have any relatives or friends. It was difficult to talk but I signaled no, I did not. The next day he came back and told me that few days prior, the hospital released a Jewish fellow who had Typhus, whose mother sat by his bed for 24 hours. He tried to locate the address of that patient but could not find it. The hospital administrator told him that they expected the mother to return in order to obtain the release documents for her son. He asked them to notify him when she gets back to the hospital. A few days later, the priest showed at my bed with the Jewish patient and his mother. She told me that she managed to survive the war with her two children, her son and a daughter. The next day she came back with warm soup and few slices of bread. I shared it with Nicolas who was lonely and hungry. His wife and daughters were back in the country when he fell ill and didn't know of his hospitalization.

The woman came back several times with a little food, walking many kilometers from the city to the hospital barracks near the Zarecze forest. It was the end of October with the first snow on the ground when I was getting better and needed to leave. I had only a shirt to wear and the woman, Chajne Oshmian was her name, brought me a Russian military coat that she purchased with her money. When I was released she invited me to her house to stay with her and her son Jacob (nick name 'yankale'). He was a few years older then me and we became fast friends. Through him I met several Jewish survivors that came in the evenings for fellowship. It was so rare and strange to find a "family" with the rest of us being sole survivors.

This is the story of the Oshmaians' survival: The family's father was a plumber in Vilna who knew the city's underground sewage system well. For many months he and a few other Jews dug a tunnel connected to the sewage system. A group of twelve, including the Oshmian family of four, survived the Ghetto's occupation, round-ups and eventual extermination, hiding beneath the street surface in the sewage system. The stench was horrific and at night they would open the manholes to get fresh air and look for food. Mr. Oshmian himself did not survive. He died from lack of air, hunger and exhaustion.

At their house I met another Jewish man, Jonah Benzionoviski, who had blond hair and blue eyes and survived the war working in a farm posing as a Pole. We struck an immediate friendship and a close bond. He was a few years older and offered for me to stay with him in a five room apartment. I said my goodbyes to Nicolas and his family and moved. The other occupants of the new apartment were injured Jewish soldiers from the Russian army that were released from the hospital.

Chapter 13

IN THE MILITARY HOSPITAL

I started to look for a better job and with the help of a new acquaintance, Shimon Dach (who lives now in Tel-Aviv and was the supervisor for a supply warehouse in a large Red Army camp outside Vilna), I found a job at the Russian Army's M.A.S.H unit. The unit commander and most of the medical staff were Jewish and I naturally found it a hospitable environment. I received a Red Army uniform, a place in the barracks and plenty to eat. I was assigned to the cultural and entertainment unit and was able to return to the apartment in Vilna on the weekends.

The commander, doctors and many of the unit's staff welcomed me with compassion and kindness when they heard that I was a holocaust survivor whose entire family was killed.

In the beginning of January 1945 the Red Army was now fighting on German soil. The military hospital was part of the army fighting the third Belarusian front. The batallions fighting the front had advanced through most of Eastern Prussia, with the exception of its provincial capital city of Kenigsberg, where heavy fighting was reported. When our M.A.S.H. unit received orders to mobilize towards the Prussian front, I was given a choice and after much personal deliberation I decided to stay with them. (This province of northeastern Prussia became a non-contiguous part of the Soviet Union and the name of its capital changed by the Russians from Kenigsberg to Kaliningrad; to this day, it is part of Russia and surrounded by the Baltic Sea to the North, Lithuania to the east and Poland to the west and south).

We arrived into Insterburg in Prussia (it is located in what became the Russian enclave of Kaliningrad and is now called Chernyak-hosk), which by then had become a total ghost town. The German population fled with little notice and left mostly everything behind them. Half of the houses were destroyed in the fighting and in the half still standing we found untouched apartments with furniture, china, clothes and even food on the tables – it seemed that whole families just left with absolutely no notice or time to prepare. Sweet revenge was indeed what I felt when I witnessed German defeat! In the basement we found civilian and military bodies from the recent fighting. Our hospital situated itself on the local university's campus. Dozens of train cars arrived with medical equipment, mobile operating units, X-ray machines, pharmaceutical inventory and food. We worked non-stop for about a week to unload the cars and set the equipment to function properly. The medical staff, nurses and administrative group were housed in comfortable apartments that were well furnished. Shortly after, we started to receive wounded soldiers from the front, mostly with serious conditions from the armored tank divisions, many of whom had severe burns.

My job, being assigned to the cultural department, was to sort and deliver mail to the soldiers as well as newspapers and books. Every evening we showed movies to the soldiers who could sit in an auditorium and inside the hospital to those who lay in bed. The screening machine had a malfunction when its belt tore and we could not get a replacement. There was no choice but to provide the rotation necessary by inserting an index finger into the wheel and turning it at a slow but constant speed for the hour and half of the movie. The person in charge of the screening and music – which were always Russian patriotic songs – was a wounded war Navy veteran, Pitkah Kurayev, who I remember as being tall and very handsome. As his helper, we spent much time together and became very close friends. Pitkah had the reputation of a ladies man, which helped him get many favors, whether it was from the kitchen ladies or the nurses that had vodka to sooth wounded soldiers. We had endless talks and I was surprised that a young fellow who was raised in the Soviet Union spoke critically of it. I was not surprised, however, that he was also an anti-Semite. I felt loyalty and gratitude to the Soviet Union in general and the Red Army in particular for saving my life and the lives of hundreds of thousands of Jews while in the midst of fighting the Nazis. Because of that loyalty that I felt to the Russians, I contemplated turning my friend in as "an enemy of the state" to the authorities but thought better of it.

The Russians were steeped in anti-Semitic sentiment fueled by generations of Czars who openly discriminated against the Jewish population. It was well known and documented that the state – prior to the revolution – sponsored or ignored many pograms in which many Jews were murdered. Jews also played a major role in first fomenting the ideology and then in the leadership of the revolutionary movement. When the Czar was toppled and the Soviet Regime established itself, Jews took leadership positions in a disproportionate ratio compared to the size of its population. That fact did little to abate the already prevalent anti-Jewish sentiment. Nevertheless, under the Soviet Union regime, anti-Semitism became illegal and punishable by law. It was explicitly forbidden to call a Jewish person "Jzeed" (similar to calling a black "nigger"), but "Jewrei" instead. But the widespread hatred towards the Jews did not go away with the passing of the law, it just wasn't as open. Meeting many Russian soldiers immediately after my liberation, I realized that the Nazi propaganda against our race had an effect on many European cultures, not limited to Germans, and that certainly included the Russians. One could hear many jokes depicting Jews as cowards who did not want to fight in the front. Even the hospital's party chairman, Major Padtakov, was openly making fun at the Jews' expense.

A very popular Soviet spy movie was circulating throughout the various hospital units. One evening we arrived at a hospital in Insterburg for viewing. Pitkah prepared the machine for the screening and left to get drunk. I was left to man the machine which meant to rotate the wheel with my finger. As I was rotating and watching the movie, it came to a part that disturbed me deeply. It depicted Abraham, a Jewish tailor, who discovered in the inside of a client's coat that he was measuring, classified military documents. As a loyal Russian, he took the documents and headed to the local police station. Sarah, his wife, ran after him to remind him that it was raining and he needed his boots. The soldiers and the wounded burst in laughter and began to sing anti-Semitic songs. I stopped the screening and began to yell at everyone: "I am a Jew who volunteered to help the Red Army in the war effort and will not tolerate any fun made at my people." Pandemonium ensued and a group of soldiers, some wielding their crutches went for me, destroying the screening machine and going for my head. Just as that happened, Pitkah – after consuming much vodka – entered the auditorium, grabbed a set of crutches from one of the soldiers, and started to hit those attacking me. A military police officer entered the hall, stopped the fighting, and arrested Pitkah and I. I was released later that night, but my friend was accused of attacking wounded soldiers and was left in the military jail. I went to see our commander Colonel Galbreich and asked him to intervene in the release of Pitkah who saved my life in the midst of a violent anti-Semitic attack. After a week, charges were dropped and my savior was released. We celebrated by drinking plenty of vodka and few days later Pitkah found another screening machine.

Our friendship grew stronger following the incident and Pitkah confessed greater respect for my people and their contribution to the war, be it mostly in the rear. Indeed, I realized as time passed that many of the engineers and scientists heading the defense industrial complex in Russia were my brethren. Moreover, the majority of the medical staff in the military hospitals as well as the logistics commanders were Jews. The entire Soviet Jewry stood firmly behind the military effort to fight the Nazi onslaught.

Chapter 14

VICTORY DAY

Spring of 1945 brought with it the intoxicating aromas of blooms, woven with encouraging news from the front. The Red Army was now fighting at the outskirts of Berlin and Allied forces took back most of western German soil with little resistance. Marshals Zookov and Koniev competed to be the first in Berlin on the targeted date of May 1st, to wave the Red flag. They barely missed their target and finally, early in the morning of May 2nd, a victory flag was hoisted on the Reichstag's top. The fall of Berlin put an end to the bloody European stage of the Second World War that took the lives of millions of people including one third of the Jewish nation. The nations comprising the Soviet Union – especially the Russians - lost tens of millions of civilians and soldiers and Europe was mostly in ruins.

There were victory celebrations in all the military units with artists performing, food served and vodka poured like water. Body and soul yearned to release the tension and suffering of the war years. I participated in the celebrations on the outside, but my heart was broken. I was left without family or a home and the whole world as I knew it had vanished. How we prayed for this moment, for the horrors to end, and now that we were liberated, we searched our souls and could not find happiness and joy. While jubilation was all around me, I felt lonely, melancholic and depressed.

Stalin decided to honor every Red Army soldier and civilian who contributed to the war effort with a victory medal. Millions would be entitled to this coveted medal that was distributed in factories, army units and hospitals in emotional ceremonies.

Every day we noticed medal ceremonies in other M.A.S.H. units in Istenburg. I began to wonder when it would be our turn. Our commanders then told us that we befell a special honor and we would receive our medals in the Kremlin by the President of the Supreme Soviet, himself, comrade Kalinin. I was very excited for the chance to be in Moscow and waited for the journey anxiously. The process of disassembling the equipment for the trip back took about a week of around the clock effort. We loaded the contents of the hospital onto the train cars and the entire unit, including the medics, nurses, doctors and administrators, got on the train headed to the capitol city. The train made a stop for a day in Vilna to replenish supplies, and I took the opportunity to seek a few old friends. I was advised by all my friends that this was not the time to take a pleasure trip to Moscow and that I must stay in Vilna. Another reason to stay was because there was a chance that Poland would issue immigration papers to the natives of Polish land prior to 1939. Those granted papers would be eligible to migrate and work in Poland. Despite their pleadings, I did not want to miss the opportunity to visit Moscow, especially with the extraordinary honor of receiving the Victory medal inside the Kremlin.

I returned to the train and told Pitkah about the meeting with my friends and how they pleaded with me not to go on with the trip. I expected his reaction to support my decision to join the unit, but, instead, he listened and kept silent.

Chapter 15

JOURNEY TO MOSCOW – THE DREAM AND THE ILLUSION

The distance from Vilna to Moscow is about 1,200 kilometers. We had many stops along the way and everywhere we saw endless traffic of military equipment and personnel heading east. At a typical stop at a town or a village, we would disembark the train, and look around the station and surrounding area. The town's square would be filled with vendors selling or trading food, clothes and articles taken from German homes. One of the items mostly sought after was, of course, vodka. At one of the stations we rested next to another train carrying Russian POWs returning home. We were amazed to see that they looked healthy, wore clean clothes and had brand new shoes. As it turned out, they were interned at a POW camp in Norway, where the local population helped feed and clothe them and even sent them off with care packages. What a contrast compared to the treatment of POWs in camps on German soil or German occupied territories, from which they returned hungry and sick.

The night prior to our arrival to Moscow I could not sleep from excitement. I was a holocaust survivor arriving in the capital city of the country that helped in defeating Nazi Germany and saved my life along with the lives of thousands of Jews. That was a miracle and indeed a dream come true. When we arrived at the suburbs of Moscow, we saw from a distance tall buildings and church steeples. The train came to a stop at a very busy train depot with many rail lines converging and hundreds of cars filled with military personnel and material. Everywhere we looked, we noticed units of the famed NKVD (the internal security forces that preceded the KGB) carrying machine guns. An officer announced that it was forbidden to leave the car, punishable by imprisonment. This peculiar "welcome" shocked us all. We anticipated representatives from the Kremlin and hotel rooms prior to the ceremony. What was the meaning of NKVD units guarding us? I decided to risk it and ran towards the head of the train to seek explanations from the hospital's command. Our unit's commander, captain Kakanin, was a resident of Moscow who had a wife and children he had not seen since he was called to duty in 1941. In the command car a few female soldiers were seated, among whom was a Jewish girl from Minsk who's name I remember to this day, Klava Ginsburg. She was the most beautiful girl in the hospital and everyone adored her beauty and kindness. From her I found the explanation I needed – our entire M.A.S.H. unit was headed to the Far East to prepare for the war against the Japanese in Manchuria. The story about medals at the Kremlin was a total lie and a deceitful plan to keep us on the train. I asked to speak to Kakanin, and he told me that the authorities would not let him go home to see his family, but instead they brought his wife and two young children for a private visit in one of the cars. This latest development caused me great anguish and I regretted deeply my decision not to stay in Vilna when I had my chance. I then knew that I simply had to find a way to leave because I possessed neither the physical nor the mental strength needed to endure another battle, this time in Southeast Asia, sorting the territorial dispute between Japan and China over Manchuria.

I asked Klava to help me obtain my identification card and a document stating that I was a civilian employed by the hospital, and once they were in my possession, I would leave at the earliest opportunity. She promised to do the best she could and that she would have a talk with Kakanin about getting the release documents. A few hours after my talk with Klava Ginsburg, the train left Moscow heading east. All the tracks were filled with hundreds of cars loaded with large numbers of military convoys, with tanks, artillery and supplies of mortar. These cars had the priority, heading to the front, and we had many hours of delays on side tracks on more then one occasion. There was much idle time and I began to exercise, running alongside the train and occasionally participating in a soccer game with others. The barter exchange was live and well, as we steadily depleted the supplies we brought from Germany. I kept the pressure on my friend Klava regarding the important documents I needed. She told me on one occasion that she spoke to Kakanin and that he refused to sign the release. About two weeks after leaving the capital, we approached the Ural mountain range. I found a moment again to speak with Klava and I told her, with tears in my eyes "I survived the extermination and I'm all alone. I have no animosity against the Japanese who harmed no Jewish people. If I can't get the papers, I will run away and risk being caught by the Russian and sent to a prison in Siberia." She said "Don't make a foolish mistake. I promise you that you will get the papers." A few days after our last talk, the train stopped at a side track with complete darkness and no sign of life anywhere. As I was sitting in the car contemplating my escape, the door opened and Klava entered. She handed me a small bundle of papers wrapped in newspaper and whispered, "Misha, I brought you all the documents you need. Be safe and good luck on your journey." I collected the few things I owned and left the train. I headed into the wooded area nearby and waited until the train started to move and then disappeared into the horizon. I was all alone with little possessions, in total darkness in the middle of the vast land of eastern Russia.

I walked along the rails for about an hour and saw a faint light at a distance. I quickly approached the source of light and as I got near, saw that it was a small shack that housed a lone rail operator. He was shocked to see me in the middle of the night at such a remote place. I introduced myself and showed him my release papers, which included, an ID card issued in Vilna, release documents from the Red Army's hospital unit, a referral to an eye clinic to treat a stubborn infection I had, food stamps for ten days and a few hundred Rubles in cash. The operator was responsible for moving the tracks when necessary to route a particular train sideways. He told me that I had a good chance to catch another train soon that was headed west back to Moscow. A couple of hours later a train pulling tree logs stopped at the exchange. I climbed on top of one of the piles of stumps and fell asleep as soon as the train started to move. I awoke as the sun came up and enjoyed the warmth after a long and cold ride at night being exposed to the wind. From the far corner of the car, I heard voices of women talking. I slowly crawled towards them and they were very surprised and a bit frightened to see me. I quickly told them who I was and the events that led me to be on this train as well as my desire to get back to Vilna my hometown. They told me that they were headed to Leningrad (St Petersburg was called Leningrad 1924-1991), the city they left during the German siege. They offered me bread and dry fish and I accepted the food eagerly as I hadn't had a thing to eat in over twenty four hours. The train stopped at one of the towns to unload its cargo and we left to ask for food from the town's officer and to look for a train heading to Moscow. At every station in the USSR during those days, one would find a container with hot water called "keapiatok" to prepare tea. The ladies had no tea but few sugar cubes that we dissolved in the hot water and we had a small meal with the provisions I received using my food stamps. The three of us decided to stick together until we reached Moscow. We hopped on several trains until we finally arrived at the capital.

My companions told me during the voyage that they had a relative residing outside of Moscow and invited me to join them for a short visit. We took the electric street car to the country, a trip of about an hour, and arrived at a beautiful modest dacha (country home) on the shore of a lake. The surrounding area was pastoral and tranquil, surrounded with water and trees. Our hosts prepared a sauna for us that was followed with a feast, the likes of which I have not seen in many years. What I remember the most was the copious amount of vodka and a platter of smoked fish and cured meat called "Zkoska" in Russian. Following a good night's rest, we returned to Moscow the next day. Originally we planned to part ways: as my train to Vilna departed from the Bialoruski gate and my Russian friends would depart from the Leningradskaya gate. My friends announced that they would not leave until they saw me boarding the train to Vilna. So the three of us arrived at the Bialoruski station and we couldn't believe the chaos. There were thousands of people crowding in every corner, on benches, corridors, passages, sidewalks and the ramps. There were uniformed personnel, injured soldiers, released soldiers and civilians. The queue to the ticket counter had hundreds of people and I soon learned a lesson about Soviet inefficiency. Apparently having a ticket for the trip was only the beginning; one also must have a "release" to win a berth on board. To obtain the release document, authorities checked for a referral from an organization or a government office. I knew that I had no chance to get to the counter to purchase the ticket and apply for the release, so we decided to take the Metro into the city center to visit Red Square and see Lenin's mausoleum. The Metro was the USSR's show piece. Every station looked palatial with marble statues and crystal chandeliers. Embossed in marble at the entrance to the Metro was the name L.M. Kaganowitz (whose full Jewish name was Leizer Ben Moshe Kaganowitz), who served as a member of the Politburo and Minister of Transportation.

We returned to the station after our quick excursion to the Red Square. I told the ladies to continue to their gate and assured them that I would be fine alone. They would have none of it and vowed not to leave me until I was on board heading to Vilna. We found a vacant bench, ate a simple meal and decided to spend the night there. I felt suffocated, being surrounded by many sweaty bodies, and needed some fresh air. I left my military coat that saved my life and a few other items I owned in a small wooden gramophone box with them, and said that I would return shortly with ice cream for everyone. I headed toward the main gate of the station and saw NKVD officials checking credentials. I thought nothing of it and showed them my papers. The soldier checking my papers called his superior and the officer asked me to follow him. He escorted me to the police section in the station's large complex. They locked me inside a cell with a group of petty criminals, some of whom were drunk and verbally abusive. A few of the thugs attacked me, found the money I had and took it all. Later, in the middle of the night I was taken to the interrogation room. My interrogator wasted no time and told me that I was accused of espionage because my papers seemed to be counterfeit. I told him that he could check the authenticity of the documents with Vilna's police and with the command of the military hospital unit. They took me back to the cell where I sat the entire next day. It was unpleasant, to say the least, to be incarcerated with scum and dangerous men.

The following night, they took me out of the cell and drove me to downtown Moscow to the NKVD's headquarters. A polite, higher ranked officer was assigned to interrogate me and it seemed to me that he could be of Jewish decent. After few questions, I told him, "Mr. Officer, it's inconceivable to accuse me of spying against the Soviet Union, a Jewish person who just recently survived the anni- hilation of his people. During the German occupation, I dreamed to see the moment of the Red Army arriving to liberate us. Now that that dream has come true you're accusing me of spying? Is it my destiny to rot in a Soviet jail after years of suffering?" He lis- tened to me without one interruption and then asked me further details about my upbringing, my family and specifically about life under the Polish regime. I chose not to share the fact that my family was upper middle class and that I attended a well known Hebrew school. When he left the room I was left to ruminate about my predicament which I created with my greedy desire to get the Medal. It was an illusion and a fraud that played on my naiveté. The officer returned to the room and by his expression I could tell that he had good news. Indeed, he gave me the travel documents I needed for the trip to Vilna shook my hand and wished me good luck.

I returned to the station and, assuming that the two women were long gone, went to the massive lost and found department, knowing that they would not leave with my possessions. Looking for my precious coat in that wooden box, I went from one window to the next sifting through what seemed like endless collection of articles. I finally gave up realizing it was like looking for a needle in a haystack. It was late at night and I went back upstairs to the waiting hall of the station, found a corner and fell asleep on the floor. In the morning I went out to the street to look for food and water. I could not believe my eyes – my two Russian friends, holding my wooden box, walked towards me, we hugged and kissed and they could not stop crying from excitement. From the moment that I left to get the ice cream, they looked for me, including going to the NKVD office at the station but could not find any information. They spent the two days sleeping in the station with my box and during the day searching for my whereabouts. Here, I discovered at its benevolent essence, the warm humanity and big heart which is the nature of the Russian people. I walked with them to the gate of the Leningrad train, we said our emotional goodbyes and I headed for the gate of the train to Vilna.

There were thousands of people waiting at the gate and I realized it was an impossible mission to get a ticket. What could I do? I needed to leave Moscow at all cost, but I had no money or food stamps. I succeeded in going through the tight security check and headed to the boarding area where I saw hundreds of soldiers including many with war injuries. I looked for an injured soldier who might need my assistance to board. I walked through the crowd and noticed a one legged soldier lying close to his crutches and few belongings. I pushed my way towards him and made a space to sit next to him. He was from Smolensk and waited for days to return home after recovering from the amputation but had difficulty advancing to and boarding the train. I knew quite well that it would be the same train heading to Smolensk and Vilna. I offered to accompany him and to help him get on the train and he acquiesced. When the train arrived, I picked up our belongings and began to plow our way through the dense crowd as my companion hopped behind me. I yelled loudly, "Let us through, I must bring this wounded soldier onto the train." When we arrived at the door of one of the cars, I tossed our bags on board, picked him up in my arms and entered. The car had no seats but three levels of wooden bunks on both sides. I lowered the soldier to the lower bunk and took the level above him. Every minute that we waited for the train to get in motion, seemed like eternity, as I feared being caught without a ticket. Finally, a whistle, and the train started to move to my great relief. During the trip we had several inspections of documents and I had no trouble with the release I received from the NKVD's officer in downtown Moscow.

At the Smolensk station, we parted ways and I continued my way to my hometown. Early the next morning I arrived at Vilna at long last.

Chapter 16

FAREWELL TO VILNA – DESTINATION POLAND

The platform at the Vilna station was crowded with many soldiers. When I exited towards the main station building, I noticed a group of civilians. To my great surprise, among them was the Ginsburg family who fled with their two daughters to the Soviet Union before the start of the war. The eldest was Chaya Ginsburg who was my classmate at Tarbut from the first grade. Her parents had an open and warm house and my friends and I would often go there after school. They stood there lost after four years of self exile returning to a ghost town with only a few Jews remaining. With the few contacts that I already had, having been in Vilna before my trip to Moscow, I helped them get oriented. We found Mr. Ginsburg's brother who was a physician in one of the clinics and he offered them shelter. When I saw her last, Chaya was a pretty thirteen year old girl but now my friend had become a young woman. We spent days reliving old memories of school and mutual friends. (Chaya still lives with her own family in a Chicago suburb to which she migrated from Europe after the war).

In accordance with an agreement between Poland and the USSR, refugees born in Polish controlled territory prior to September 1, 1939, had the right to migrate to Poland. I registered for the immigration papers with hundreds of other Jewish survivors, and, in September 1945 after the Jewish New Year, I boarded a train heading to Warsaw. I decided to go there because I heard rumors that there was a group of Vilna refugees who were deported to labor camps in Estonia and had survived the war, mostly in northern Poland and Germany. I had hoped to find my father, who was deported to Estonia, among the survivors. For years I carried with me the intuition that one day I would see my father again. I dreamed of him and our meeting many nights and I even went to several Gypsy clairvoyants who read my future, some analyzing the palm of my hand and others reading cards who all confirmed my dreams of reuniting with my father. One Gypsy told me that he was alive but very ill and that there was a good chance for us to meet soon.

The day I left Vilna was very hot and the station was crowded with thousands of people. I left my hometown with a group of friends and acquaintances, among whom was Jonah Benzionovski, who I met and shared an apartment with after the liberation. We waited for hours to board the freight train. I went out to get a cold drink and when I proceeded to pay, I recognized the cashier as the engineer Poonsky, who was a tenant at our building. He worked with my father during the Ghetto period at the lumber mill, the location from which they were kidnapped and deported to Estonia. He told me that my father died at the labor camp from exhaustion, hunger and illness. My last hope to find a surviving family member had vanished for good. I realized then that I was all alone in the world. I weighed whether to cancel the move to Poland, but I wanted to run away from this cursed and bloody soil. I returned to the train sobbing with grief and my friends were shocked to see me join them in an obvious devastated state of mind.

We arrived at Warsaw in complete darkness and desolation. The train station's main building was a heap of rubble. I found a Polish worker as we disembarked and asked him what the situation was like in Poland in general and in Warsaw in particular. He told me that the Poles were licking their wounds and were hopeful that they would slowly rebuild. He then said that the problem he saw was the wave of Jewish displaced persons (DP) arriving from the USSR, estimated at hundred of thousands. I took great offense in his remarks and told him sarcastically that from what I'd heard the Jews were coming in the millions and were likely to flood all of Poland. Not realizing that I was Jewish myself and was mocking him, he crossed himself and said, "God help us." This "warm" welcome on Polish soil – where 90% of its three and a half million pre-war Jewish population perished – was not what I expected.

We left Warsaw and continued to Lodz, a few hours ride. At the Lodz station, we met representatives of its Jewish community who were there to assist with lodging and general DP issues. Lodz was one of the few cities in Poland, similar to Krakow that survived the war with little physical damage. It's electric and water grids were functioning normally, and its cafes and restaurants filled with customers. The sharp contrast from the devastation of Warsaw and to lively city life of Lodz seemed eerie to me.

As I mentioned, one of my companions was Jonah Benzionovski. Before we left Vilna, he succeeded in finding the attic where his father hid money, clothes and valuable coins. Most of the paper disintegrated but there was enough for him to purchase new clothes for both of us, some vodka and other garments he hoped to sell in Poland. We went to the market in Lodz and were able to sell what we brought from Vilna. Selling in the market, we encountered and later joined a group of Jewish folks who smuggled merchandise from areas evacuated by Germans in order to earn some money.

Chapter 17

KIBBUTZ DROR AND THE ZIONIST MISSION

As I was walking in the center city of Lodz one morning, I ran into Mr. Sheftel, one of my teachers at Tarbut. The meeting was very emotional to both of us and we hugged warmly, caught up on events since the beginning of the war. When he heard that I was involved with a group of guys dealing with the black market, he was disappointed and lectured me that it was unacceptable for a Tarbut student who speaks Hebrew to be involved with unscrupulous activities. You must join the Zionist cause immediately, he said, and get involved with worthy educational activity. I accepted his challenge with no hesitations and he took me to a building on 18 Polodniova Street, which housed the group that started the Kibbutz Lochmei Hagetaot – Fighters of the Ghettos.

It should be explained that the rebuilding of the future State of Israel and the dream of returning the Jewish people from the Diaspora after two thousand years, known as the Zionist movement, began in the late 19th century and continued at the start of the 20th century with the establishments of Kibbutzim in Palestine – as it was known before Israel became a state in 1948. The concept of the Kibbutz embodied many aspirations and historical currents that the Jews in Europe experienced, such as Socialism, Agrarianism and Zionism. It was natural for the pioneers at the budding settlements in Israel to send representatives to Europe, where most of the worlds Jewry lived, in order to recruit them for the cause and encourage them to migrate to the promise land.

This effort intensified immediately after the war with hundreds of thousands of homeless Jewish refugees looking for a new start far from the torched soil of the European continent. Typically these representatives of Israeli Kibbutz, financed with seed money of non-governmental organizations, searched for enough refugees, men and women to start a seed group that would eventually make the voyage to Israel and join the settlement. These efforts became increasingly difficult with the blockade of the shores of Palestine by the British authorities, a situation so dire for the homeless refugees that many resorted to desperate measures, legal and not, to reach the land of Israel.

In front of the house stood two young Jewish men with guns to protect its inhabitants. Once inside I heard Hebrew songs, laughter and wonderful spirit of a distant past. There were banners in Yiddish and Hebrew, flags and a large map of "Eretz Israel" – the land of Israel. I stood there speechless for a moment remembering the Zionist fervor that permeated Tarbut when I was younger.

I went to the room where the leadership committee established their office, introduced myself and answered questions about my background and education. It was comforting to learn that many of the leaders came from Vilna and Lita. They asked me to join the Kibbutz and I immediately accepted. They gave me a bed in a room with several other fellows and told me that I would join them to work the very next day. My group worked in a winery that was under Jewish ownership for many years. The winery's owner survived the concentration camps and returned to Lodz and reclaimed his family's business. The sign outside the winery read in Polish: Winery and Distillery Bacchus. Our group joined other workers who were Polish in various manual chores. Occasionally, we would taste the liquor and would also bring wine to the house for the Shabbat Kiddush. Part of our job was to distribute the wine and liqueur, using rickshaws – with no horses or vehicles available – to local restaurants and hotels. In comparison to the other jobs or chores given to Kibbutz members, our job was easier and had opportunities to earn extra cash. Consequently, tension grew between us. Once a week, local farmers arrived to load the waste material from the winery to feed their animals and left us fresh butter, cheese and smoked meats in exchange. We brought the food to the house and feasted with these excellent provisions that were much better then the meager daily food we had. There were also plenty of spirits available from the winery, and many nights, the group stayed late sampling the products. The leadership of the Kibbutz was concerned about the deteriorating discipline and general party mode and quickly moved to disband the winery group. A few members of the group left the Kibbutz and stayed as hired hands in the winery. I accepted a position with a start-up committee in Krakow to establish a new Kibbutz called "Dror" (Sparrow).

I left Lodz by train to Krakow to join my new group in the middle of a very cold winter of 1946. The train was not heated and many of the windows were shattered. By the time I arrived, I was close to freezing. I walked several kilometers in the snow to find the address of the house given to me. I found several members already there and they sat me close to a stove with hot tea and some vodka. After a good night sleep, I met with the rest of the group who told me about our assignments. The leader of the Kibbutz was a graduate of a young pioneer movement (H'chalutz ha' tzaeer) who was scheduled to go to Israel as the war broke. He escaped from

Germany to Russia and soon after liberation, returned to Poland and resumed his activities with the Zionist youth movement. Similar to my own journey west to Poland, many survivors arrived daily by train, escaping or being forced out by the post-war Soviet Union which became increasingly inhospitable under Stalin's regime. Our job was to fan out to the various train stations, locate Jewish refugees and provide them aid and shelter. Another location to find Jewish survivors was the local Jewish community center. I stood in front of one such building all day trying to recruit young folks to join the Kibbutz. Within weeks, our group grew to a hundred and with no room left, we searched for another location to house the growing number of new arrivals.

According to a post-war agreement, the Soviet Union received a vast portion of land from eastern Poland in exchange for German territories it conquered between the rivers Oder and Nysa. The majority of the German inhabitants there fled, fearing the Russians, and those who stayed were forced to leave their homes by the Poles. Whole towns remained completely empty following this human migration. It was an opportunity to settle Polish citizens who received apartments that were completely furnished and in some cases, had clothes and basements with provisions and heating coal. It was in these cities that we found the space we needed for dozens of groups of young men and women.

In addition to our efforts to absorb those arriving from the USSR by trains, we looked for released prisoners of concentration camps – most of whom were women – who were housed in temporary absorption centers in the Russian controlled zone of Germany. There were also many young women and men from Lita, Latvia and the USSR who did not qualify for Polish citizenship, and therefore whose entry to Poland was forbidden. It was one of our missions to find a way to smuggle these women into Polish territory and absorb them in one of the Kibbutzim groups. I was one of the operatives with proper documentation that went back east to find surviving women in need of a home and bring them west. On a typical mission, several of us would meet a group of five or so women at a rendezvous location according to a prearranged communication, escort them to the local train station, bribe a guard or a soldier and board a freight car headed to Krakow. Arriving in Krakow, we brought them to the Kibbutz house and found them shelter with one of the groups in the area towns.

The post-war period was very fluid and chaotic in all aspects; the security situation, political instability, structural ruin and obviously personal tragedy. Poland was ruled by the communist party whose various security and military forces were flexing their respective power. The exiled Polish government, residing in London, exerted its influence with several ministers in the government. There were signs of relative personal freedom which provided fertile condition for political activities. All Zionist organizations renewed their prewar activities except two that were outlawed, the Bei'tar and the Revisionist. The anti-Zionist "Bond" party espoused, as it did before the war, permanent Jewish community life to be encouraged in Poland. They too, made an effort to recruit surviving souls to their ranks. There was a wide Jewish support for the communist party in Poland, which was not sympathetic to the Zionist cause of migrating to Palestine and the establishment of the Israeli state. This conflict, which manifested itself in harassments against our organization, among others, made it clear that Poland may no longer provide the temporary safe heaven we hoped for. Moreover, the leader of the Zionist groups assessed that time was running out before Poland fell completely under the Soviet sphere of influence. Consequently, a massive migration movement of the Kibbutzim groups, the infamous "Flight" operation – organized by Israeli and local operatives – began to take place. Tens of thousands of Jewish refugees left Poland for American controlled zones, including Austria and Germany. The two main crossings were the Czech border in the south and the port city of Szczecin in the north – the latter being a natural choice as it was the largest seaport in Poland and our goal was to ship as many refugees by sea to the shores of Israel.

The "Dror" Kibbutz movement was connected ideologically to the United Kibbutz organization (H'Kibbutz H'Meuchad) which was the strongest in Poland. The leaders of the movement were survivors of the Warsaw Ghetto uprising: Isaac Zucherman and Tzvia Luvetkin. Politically, our movement identified itself with the United Labor group that split from the Mapaie party, whose leader, Isaac Tabenkin, was very influential with the Holocaust survivors because of his role in calling for an armed resistance against the British Mandate in Palestine and its Arab population. We also greatly admired the Palmach (pre-curser to the Israeli Defense Forces) who leaned on the United Kibbutz party for support and recruits.

Poland, at that juncture, was filled with strong anti-Russian and anti-Semitic sentiment. Chief among the haters was the Catholic priesthood whose influence upon the populace was significant. Jews were attacked physically and some murdered when returning to their home towns to reclaim their family's homes or property. We heard of instances of Poles tossing Jews off moving trains to their deaths while making their journey back "home" after liberation. To my knowledge, Poland was the only country in Europe where Jews were murdered after the Nazi defeat. The new Polish Administration relied on the Soviet military to provide security and could not prevent terrorist attacks of armed nationalistic gangs. The government had several old guard Jewish communists in ministerial positions whose existence only intensified the hatred towards our people. It was only an excuse, however, as the hatred against the Jewish population was prevalent before the war and during the German occupation; many Poles collaborated with the murderers and stole Jewish property. In July 1946, Polish underground members murdered 39 Jews in the town of Kielce. The Polish Prime Minister summoned the leaders of the Jewish communities and told them that, because of the horrible massacre, he would open Polish borders for three days and allow those who wished to leave the country. Thousands of Jews took advantage of the offer and fled mostly to Austria and Germany. Before my departure from Poland, the Kibbutz sent me as a representative to the first "Dror" conference taking place in Lodz. There was also a delegation from Israel that provided the bulk of the speakers at the seminars. The graduates of the conference were sent to the Kibbutzim, which were present in most cities in Poland as counselors.

They sent me to the city of Wroclaw in southwestern Poland, which had a large Kibbutz located in a building that belonged to the Jewish community before the war. I was responsible for the cultural and education programs of the group. With my fluency in Hebrew, I started classes and taught the language to hundreds of participants. Wroclaw was mostly destroyed during the war, but in the quarters still standing, hundreds of families returning from Russia found shelter. Our mission was to raise the awareness of the children and youth, outside the Kibbutzim circle, of Jewish and Zionist issues of the day. The study group I was leading had about 50 young participants. The adults were invited to evenings of lectures and sing-a-longs, and on Shabbat we organized Shachrit prayer with hundreds of participants.

Our activities raised the suspicion and anger of the local Communist party. An official arrived at our office and summoned me to appear in front of the head of the region's Communist party. I arrived at their office at the time ordered and the Secretary welcomed me politely. After few minutes of small talk he revealed the purpose of the meeting. "Listen," he said, "I am Jewish too but no one knows it. We are facing unrest from the general population who does not trust and support the new Polish government. The Jewish groups need to help us to establish stability and confidence in the party and, knowing your influence in your community, I'm asking you to stop all Zionist activities and join our ranks." He proceeded to promise me advancement, economic incentives and a free university education in return for my collaboration. I immediately told him that, although we supported the regime, I would not stop my mission to help survivors fulfill their dream to migrate to Israel after the bloody years of the war. Before I left, he asked me to appeal to the Kibbutz community for our participation in a large demonstration at the city center square in honor of a visit by Wladislav Gomoulka, the Secretary General of the People's Party – who was also the Minister in charge of the liberated territories. I agreed and convinced the four Kibbutz groups in the city to mobilize their members to participate in the demonstration. At the day of the event we gathered, 500 strong, at the city square with thousands of others. As soon as Mr. Gomoulka finished his speech, a priest joined him on stage and began a Mass. Everyone kneeled and, stunned, we remained standing. The crowd began to yell anti-Semitic epithets and threats at us. It was a humiliating and an embarrassing event, especially because it was organized under the auspices of the People's party that espoused solidarity and freedom to all people.

We returned, convinced that our time in Poland was short amidst such strong anti-Jewish sentiment in the population and its leadership. We knew that we must make a proactive move. We prepared to flee and organized everyone onto trains heading to a town on the Czech border. We met with operatives of relief organizations that assisted Jewish refugees who needed to find safety. After spending the night with the local Kibbutz, we fanned in the town and gathered supplies for the journey. Our group was comprised of young men, women, whole families with children and a few elders. The next night, we started the trek on foot toward the tree covered hills near the border. Complete silence was imposed and smoking was not allowed. The road was treacherous. Many people were too weak to climb had to be carried by the stronger among us. As the sun rose, our companions who navigated the hills announced that we were on Czech soil close to the town of Nachod at the Hradec Kralove region. We marched right into the main street of this fourteenth century town and could not believe our eyes. On both sides of the street, locals began to gather with welcoming smiles on their faces, offering us bread, water and sweets. I could not comprehend how only few kilometers divided people with such opposite mentalities as the Poles and the Czechs; the former being so spiteful and the latter so hospitable.

After a short stay in Nachod, we boarded a train headed to the capitol city of Prague. Representatives of the Red Cross and the Israeli Youth movement met us at the station with tea and sandwiches, and shortly after we departed to Bratislava, the capitol of Slovakia. When we arrived, we boarded trucks that took us to the center of town. There, we were directed to a civic building with a large hall that was crowded with thousands of refugees in horrid sanitary conditions. We were terribly disappointed with our destination following many days of wandering since we left Poland. To the many thousands of refugees that transferred through this transition facility, it was not so fondly known as the "flee hotel." Our next destination was Vienna, and from the Slovak-Austrian border we had to march on foot. In order to get there, we had to cross over Soviet controlled territory that stretched over a few dozen kilometers. It was a delicate situation because citizens of the Eastern Bloc were forbidden to travel in the American controlled zone. Red Army units patrolled the area intensively. So close to the termination of hostilities in the continent, Europe's roads and passage ways were filled with displaced persons of many nationalities and various destinations. The organizers of our exodus instructed us to pretend to be Greek Jews who were allowed in Soviet areas and not to speak a word of Yiddish, Polish or Russian. Further, when spoken to, they instructed us to simply recite passages from the Bible or to sing Psalm songs. To everyone's great dismay, our leaders instructed us all to discard and destroy all documents, photographs or any items from our homes that may reveal our origin. In hindsight, this was especially cruel and probably unnecessary and we lost the last tangible connection to our homes, families and past. A few people refused to follow this unusual order and our guards took them with a promise to return, but few received them back.

Finally, we arrived in Austria, which was under American protectorate, and felt great sense of relief. Our first destination in Vienna was the Rothschild hospital that already housed thousands of DP's. A few days later, we were instructed again to move to the northeastern town of Linz, on the banks of the Danube River. We were taken to a prison camp that was surrounded with barbed wire and had several guard towers. Even though we were free and the guards were American GI's, that site brought back unpleasant memories of a not so distant past. An American Officer greeted us and politely told us that we were under the American Army's command. He told us that for now we could not leave the camp and basic military discipline was expected of us. Then he added something that shocked us deeply: we were sharing the camp with POW's, including German SS officers, and we were expected to leave them completely alone. I asked the officer, as the leader of the Kibbutz, to speak to him privately. He invited me to his office, gave me a cigarette and asked me what the matter was. I explained that we were holocaust survivors and we refused to share this camp with SS murderers. Furthermore, we would not agree to be held as prisoners. He called his superiors and told them that the Jewish refugees refused to remain inside the camp. Shortly after, a Jeep arrived at his office with several American officers. One of them was the unit's chaplain who was a Rabbi. He spoke Yiddish to me and promised that within twenty four hours, the Germans POW's would be moved to a prison camp. We would have total freedom of movement because the camp's command was transferred from the

American command to UNRA (United Nations Refugee Agency), and would be operated as a refugee facility, not a prison. After they treated us with DDT, we got into our barracks and had a meal.

The accommodations were clean, in sharp contrast to the DP facilities we experienced in Bratislava and Vienna. It was the first night of real rest I'd had in a very long time. In the morning a group representing the Linz' Jewish community came to visit us and I was invited to meet the leadership of a neighboring DP camp in the Bindermichael part of town. The refugees inhabiting that camp were mostly survivors of Austrian concentration camps. In order to find housing for the ever growing stream of refugees, the American army confiscated an entire quarter of the town and offered comfortable housing for the survivors. They lived in relative luxury and received excellent food from the American Joint Organization, to the great envy of the local population who had difficulty getting fresh provisions. We witnessed, with considerable glee, the locals fight over scraps of food that the refugees discarded.

More Jewish refugees kept arriving from Poland into Austria and Germany, and dozens of DP camps were quickly erected to absorb them. The Non-Government Organizations (NGO's) could not handle the huge humanitarian crisis that included the need for shelter, nutrition and medical attention. I became involved in facilitating the assistance that was needed for the newly arriving refugees from the local community. I then established an organizational structure within the refugee groups to allocate the food and other supplies. The support and dedication we received from the local community and the NGO's was exemplary. Representatives from Israel arrived, plotting transfer routes in the direction of Italy and Germany – both countries had major sea ports. After about a month in the DP camp outside Linz, we were instructed to board a train heading to Bavaria in Germany.

Michael on the right with friends from Kibbutz Dror, Lodj 1945

Chapter 18

DP CAMP WASSERHALFINGEN
IN GERMANY

We arrived at a temporary refugee camp, erected by the American
army that absorbed thousands of Jews and dozens of Kibbutzim
groups, similar to ours, that made the voyage from Poland. From
the neighboring Munich, a representative of Jewish NGO's and
an Israeli coordinator named Abram Gevelber came to visit us.
It became clear from their assessment that we were to stay there
a short while and move to another camp inside the city that used
to be a German Army camp which was under the UNRA control.
Despite the crowded conditions, the camp was kept clean and well
organized. Every morning I took the street car to the Dror headquarters in Munich for meetings pertaining to the movement of
and caring for the refugees. Mr. Golber asked me to join the leadership committee in Munich but I refused to leave the group with
which I traveled from Poland and chose to transfer with them.

The monumental task of caring for millions of refugees arriving
at the American controlled zone meant life, death or continued
suffering to the many helpless. In general, we were termed as DP
(displaced persons) and included many diverse groups: Lithuanians, Ukrainians, Latvians and Estonians who collaborated with
the Nazis and had to flee the USSR fearing retribution, hundreds
of thousands of Russians released from hard labor camps who
refused to return and, of course, Jews who survived the camps
and Ghettos. The American Military Administration bore the big-
gest burden with the help of UNRA and the American JDC (Joint

Distribution Committee, established in 1914 to "serve the needs of Jews throughout the world, particularly where their lives as Jews are threatened or made more difficult").

In order to provide temporary housing to the millions of refugees, the organizers emptied German Army facilities and, when that wasn't enough, forced out whole neighborhoods of Germans from their homes. I was sent with my group of about few hundred Jews to one such neighborhood, called Wasserhalfingan that used to accommodate the laborers of a nearby locomotive plant. The houses were two stories high, each containing four apartments that were furnished modestly and had hot water, heat and a gas stove. Every apartment had a small parcel of land to cultivate vegetables. Many of the Germans that were forced out volunteered to provide the labor for that task. The neighborhood had a population of about two thousand Jews which spread over many city blocks. The management of the camp was entrusted to its inhabitants and a committee comprised of the various groups became the governing body. A central committee was elected with the Poalei Zion movement obtaining the majority of the votes. My friend Motel Silverstein, whom I knew from Wroclaw, Poland, was elected Chairman and I accepted the Secretary General position of the camp. The camp was completely autonomous and our responsibilities included all services: medical, education, security, sanitation, supplies, food and entertainment. To provide the needed medical attention, the clinic had full time doctors and nurses. In the school building that was confiscated we ran a school that provided daily classes to hundreds of children of all grades. Most of the teachers were camp residents with university degrees and we received help from teachers sent from Israel. The World ORT Organization established a vocational school that taught carpentry, machine shop and metal smithing. For security and order, we established a small Jewish police force with most of the members having been in the Red Army. We tailored uniforms that had a Star of David on the hats and sleeves. The logistics department was responsible for the warehousing and distribution of our food. The basic ingredients we survived on – milk, bread, flour, eggs, sugar and oil – were provided by the local German civic authority. An additional source of food was UNRA, which supplied canned fish and processed meat. The JDC spoiled us with occasional treats of coffee, chocolate and cigarettes.

The urban German population lived in terrible density receiving a ration of 800 calories per day – in contrast to the 2000 calories rationed to the DP's. The hardship experienced by the Germans created a thriving black market where all personal belongings were exchanged for food, including art, jewelry and even collections of stamps. Young German women worked as domestic helpers in Jewish apartments for food alone. German youth offered to drive us on tri-cycles from the Aalen train station located five kilometers from the camp for a few hundred Marks (a packet of cigarettes in the black market was about 120 Marks). In time, the normal rations of canned food became redundant and soon a butcher shop complete with a Jewish orthodox butcher from Hungry opened up. The cows, bartered with local farmers, were smuggled at night into the camp for slaughter and those able to pay, had fresh meat.

The day to day management of the camp was more than a full time job. I had to keep constant communication with the American military Governor, UNRA's liaison and the mayor of the town in order to ensure the camp was functioning properly. My mentor, Motle Silverstein who was the camp's general manager, along with his wife Rivkah, adopted me like a son. I knew Motle since the days of Kibbutz Dror in Wroclaw and we stayed together from that time. Even though he was not an educated man, he was an excellent administrator and ruled the camp forcefully and efficiently. During that time, I developed an effective sense for public relations, keen talent for persuasion and achieving goals while treating everyone fairly. A few examples of some of the success I had working for the camp were: securing better transportation to move the DP's from the camp into town, loosening of the red tape pertaining to marriage ceremonies and providing better entertainment.

The camp was certainly not monolithic and I met, for the first time in my life, ultra-orthodox Jews wearing hard black hats and, during the Sabbath, a special fedora with a fur rim called "schtreimle." In Vilna, the Jews were known as the "misnagdim", the opponents – meaning those that oppose the Chasidic strand of observant Judaism – who dressed similarly to the general population and wore very short sideburns. Despite the fact that most of the refugees were not strictly observant, we kept a Jewish character in the day to day life at the camp and did not allow vehicles to enter during the Shabbat. Two strong forces exerted the most influence on the camp's population: on the one hand we had a synagogue, mikveh (ritual bath) and a Talmud learning center, all to accommodate the observant Jews, and on the other, the Zionist movements were most dominant in our camp, as they were in all DP camps, which was evident in the prevalent sentiment for the migration to Eretz Israel. Indeed, a constant stream of refugees made the illegal "aliya", ascending as it was known, into Israel with the help of Israeli operatives (the British Mandate in Palestine had a strict quota for the number of Jews allowed to immigrate). Many yearned to go to America, Canada and other countries as well, but kept their desires discreet lest they would be regarded as traitors. For many years, we were steeped in the cause of re-erecting Israel after 2000 years of exile and now, after the holocaust, that desire was more intense then ever before. Furthermore, Jewish life in the Diaspora, no matter where it was, was deemed as negative and destructive to the Jewish spirit and way of life by those who believed in the Homeland dream.

Among the camp's 2,000 residents, there was a group that did not make us proud, nor helped our image, who preferred to get engaged with unscrupulous activities. They were involved in thievery from the Germans and the refugees inside the camp. Our own police force had to confront them forcefully including incarceration and expulsion. One of our guiding principles in leading the camp was to practice high degree of transparency and ethics. Since most supplies including clothes and food were donated, fair distribution to all was critical. When it came to special needs, we clearly posted the names of those qualified to receive additional supplies or special meals due to medical conditions. I discovered early on that public work had its gratification but also its share of disappointments and criticism.

I found myself at the age of 22, holding the position of Secretary General of our large DP camp, a well known and respected person within the refugee population. In my leadership position, I was in the center of action of all aspects of the camp's life. I worked around the clock in supervision, training and coordinating the activities of the departments of health, social services and cultural affairs. I gave speeches in dozens of rallies given in many camps and towns in Germany in front of thousands of refugees, organized by the Kibbutz Movement to kindle the Zionist spirit of the attendees.

But at the peak of my success, I experienced a deep emotional crisis. I knew as a kid, that several siblings of my parents migrated to America at the turn of the century, during the mass Jewish migration to North America that was the result of worsening conditions and programs in Russia. I inquired with the Jewish NGO's who provided family search services about the whereabouts of surviving aunts and uncles. The search resulted in finding an uncle, my mother's brother, named Phillip Socket who lives in Los Angeles. I sent him a letter, describing who I was and what I went through. After about a month, A Jewish officer in the American army came to see me and told me that he made a contact with my uncle. He said that his research found that Mr. Socket was a wealthy businessman in LA and that he was willing to sponsor me and arrange the documentation needed for immediate immigration. The officer notified me that he would take care of my transfer to the United States as long as I accepted the offer from my uncle. I replied that I was steadfast in my decision to immigrate to Israel and would not consider my uncle's invitation. In addition to Mr. Socket, I later found other relatives in the US that left Eastern Europe either before I was born or when I was very young. Both my parents came from large families, – my father had eight siblings and my mother had three – and it was not uncommon at the turn of the twentieth century for those who could afford the voyage to migrate to America who opened its borders at the time. As a result of the search I also received an emotional letter from my aunt Keidy, from my father's side, who lived in Brooklyn and she too urged me to join her and her warm family in NY. She told me to my great delight that my cousin Genya who escaped the H.K.P camp was alive and well and resided with her. Soon after I found that my father's two other sisters were alive and resided in Minneapolis and New York. The existence of relatives who welcomed me over the ocean, in contrast to the fact that I knew not a person in Israel, presented me with a very difficult dilemma. I was torn between my deep desire to be among my remaining kin and my strong belief in and commitment to the Israeli cause. I knew that in Israel there existed a desperate struggle between the small Jewish settlers and the large Palestinian population, and if I went there, my struggle would continue. America promised a calmer and more comfortable life.

Representatives of the Haganah (precursor to the ADF) established recruitment and training centers in Germany, using old German Army facilities, in preparation for the migration to Israel and the enlistment to its war effort. The leadership of the DP camps joined the recruitment efforts and did not hesitate to pressure the youth, bordering on coercion, to join the movement. In our camps, dozens of young men and women – mostly single survivors – signed up and transported to training centers. More difficult was the task of recruiting youth still living with their parents who refused to send their kids to the raging war in Israel. In the midst of this campaign, I was still struggling to decide which direction to go, Israel or America. Slowly, rumors of my plans to "defect" to America spread through the camp like wildfire, with the proof that indeed I was yet to sign up. The camp's population grew angry with the thought that one of their leaders was going to America, while their children were sent to war, and the situation became unbearable and unattainable. Most of my friends in the secretariat who were older and more mature, told me privately, don't hesitate for a moment, go to the United States to be with your relatives where you could get an education. They reminded me that no one was waiting for me in Israel and my efforts and status at the DP camp would surely go unnoticed. Israel, they said, would not go away and I could always fulfill my dream and make the Aliyah in later years. To make things more complicated and tempting, I received care packages from my relatives in America with clothes, letters and Dollars.

An officer form the Haganah's command, who was in charge of all recruitment efforts in Germany, invited me for a talk. He told me this: "Michael, I don't want to pressure you to sign for recruitment and I am aware of your personal dilemma. But you must understand that your indecision has become an obstacle to our efforts. Many potential recruits," he continued, "Use your situation as an excuse not to join. You have two choices: either join or you must leave the camp immediately." After the talk I couldn't sleep all night long thinking about my crossroad – where would I go? This decision would shape my destiny for the rest of my life!

I got up in the morning with a firm decision; I had to play the card that was dealt to me. Previously I spoke in dozens of rallies making fiery speeches about the importance of Eretz Israel. I denounced sharply those who left the Zionist camp and chose life in the Diaspora. I have no choice but to remain true to my own words and join myself. I phoned the Haganah officer and told him of my decision.

I left the camp that was my home and which I helped lead and arrived at the Haganah's training camp. There, I joined hundreds of young men and women that shared deep ideology for the re-erection of Israel and a commitment to help in its war of independence.

Michael, Wasserhalfingen, Germany, 1947

A visit to the kindergarten at Wasserhalfingen

Michael speaks at a rally for Israel, Germany 1947

Michael as Wasserhalfingen's General Secretary

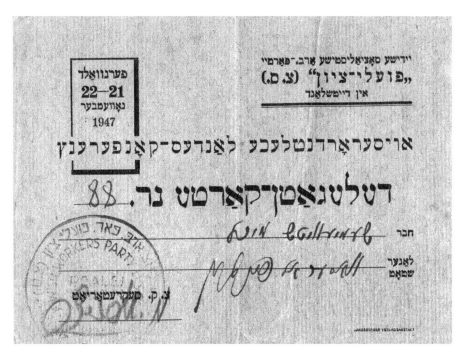

Michael's participant card, national convention of "Poaley Tzion"
Germany, 1947

Michael's voting card, International Zionist Convention 1948

Chapter 19

ERETZ ISRAEL

The historic announcement of the Declaration of Independence of the new state of Israel came on the 15th of May 1948 while I was still at the training camp. We celebrated the event with ceremonies, marches and dances. Shortly after, counselors from the Haganah briefed us on the process of making the awaited voyage to Israel. One night, a convoy of trucks with the American army star on its doors pulled into the camp. We boarded the trucks and traveled all night to a border town between Germany and France. There, we boarded a train that took us to the port city of Marseille in the south of France.

Close to the city was a large absorption camp holding thousands of young refugees waiting for a ship to ferry them across the Mediterranean Sea to the shores of Israel. Our group that arrived from Germany had about 500 men and women recruits, and I was nominated to be the person in charge. A few days later I was called to a briefing at the camp's command with the other chiefs and we were told that in a matter of days we would get the moving orders. We would board trucks that would take us to a small port few kilometers outside Marseille where a ship was waiting for us. The camp's commander told us that heavy fighting was reported from Palestine in all fronts and that our groups were anxiously anticipating to augment the fighting force. He further told us that the ship would carry 1,200 people. He nominated two of us to represent the immigrants. One person spoke French and Arabic and the other was me, representing the Polish and Eastern Europeans. Few days later at midnight a convoy of trucks arrived, and, as planned, we orderly and quietly boarded them. After a short drive we arrived at a dock and saw our ship. In fact, it was not a ship but a large boat designed for river voyage. We boarded the vessel and discovered that this excursion would be far from luxurious. In the cabin of the boat they built triple layer bunks in long rows and we had to cram everyone, literally, like sardines to fit. Even before we left the pier the heat and lack of space was terribly suffocating. The Captain announced instructions in Hebrew and I translated to Yiddish, Polish and Russian. He was specific about discipline, cleanliness, food and water allocation and safety procedures. He also, to our surprise, warned us about British air reconnaissance flights searching for boats carrying refugees to Israel, as the British Mandate had ended with the declaration of the state. In the morning everyone spilled up to the open decks to breathe fresh air and the crew, worried about the boat tipping, had to spread the crowd evenly for better balance.

The Captain and some of his crew were Jewish sailors from the American Navy who volunteered for this mission. As one of the two leaders, I was attached to the Captain and was invited to reside and dine with the crew – a big improvement from the cramped condition in the cabin below where the refugees suffered from exhaustion and sea sickness. Part of my responsibility was to listen to electronic communication from Israel, and I was kept informed with up to date information about the fighting with the Arabs. Twice daily I broadcasted throughout the boat in three languages the news from our homeland fighting its War of Independence.

We sailed for a week in rough seas. Everyone, though totally exhausted, kept searching the eastern horizon for the shores of Israel to appear. The Captain, who I admired as an exceptional human being, called the leaders to his cabin and informed us that we would not be able to continue to our destination because a cease fire had been reached between the fighting parties. Under a UN agreement and with its supervision in all ports, no new immigration was allowed to proceed. We floated for two days outside the territorial waters of Israel. It seemed like an eternity. Our collective nerves have been pulled to the breaking point and we experienced tension mixed with anticipation.

Early in the morning of July 11, 1948 we announced that the fighting resumed and that we were making landfall later that day in the port city of Haifa. All the passengers that could stand on their feet gathered on deck looking at the horizon for the first sign of land. When we caught the first glimpse of the hills of Carmel, awash with sunlight, our disheveled group of about a thousand refugees broke into the Israeli anthem the Hatikvah (the hope). Tears of joy poured out of my eyes and I felt a strong jolt of supreme elation and personal triumph.

Chapter 20

JOINING THE HAGANAH

We docked at the Haifa port and began to disembark the sick and disabled according to a process we had planned during the voyage. Inside the port buildings waiting for us were military personnel, Jewish Agency representatives and a crowd of curious people. I noticed a civilian holding a sign bearing my name. I approached him and he said that he represented the Secretariat of the Kibbutzim movement and he was there to take me to Kibbutz Yagur where I was to join the leadership of the Dror group including Yitzchak Zukerman and Tzvia Lubetkin. (Mr. Zukerman was the commander of the Warsaw Ghetto resistance which operated alongside the Polish underground called Antek. He was credited for supplying weapons to the Ghetto and hideouts for fighters after the defeat of the Ghetto's uprising. Ms. Lubetkin was a unit commander in the Warsaw Ghetto uprising and after the war she and Mr. Zukerman married. Their granddaughter was the first female fighter pilot in the Israeli Air-Force). I thanked him and said that I would not leave the group I met in Europe for the purpose of joining the Haganah and helping with the war effort. I returned to my group and we boarded buses that took us to an absorption facility near the village of Pardes Hannah. When we got there we found thousands of immigrants including families with children. The next day officers from the Israeli Defence Forces (IDF) arrived to begin to sort and register those eligible for recruitment. Together with several hundreds of fresh and young recruits, I arrived at the military welcome camp in Beit Leed.

In the camp, we found thousands of new conscripts from all corners of the Diaspora. Besides the languages familiar to me, Yiddish, Polish, Russian, Romanian and Hungarian, I heard the tongues of North Africa and French. We went through the medical examinations and I received the highest physical profile possible. Later, I was issued my military card and thereby became an Israel soldier. Prior to the swearing ceremony and issuance of uniforms they gave us a 48 hour leave. A group of us hitched hiked to Tel-Aviv. Friends I knew from Wasserhalfingen, arranged to visit relatives who had lived in Tel-Aviv since before the war and were considered "old-timers." It was the middle of July and Tel-Aviv was steaming hot. We had to walk for many kilometers to find the various neighborhoods and, finally, exhausted, had to find a simple hotel by the sea to spend the night. As soon as we fell asleep, the sirens started to howl and we were told to run to the basement because of an Egyptian raid. The next day, we finally arrived at the apartment of the first relative and our visit was shocking and disappointing. I dreamed of a warm reunion with Jewish brothers who had waited with opened arms and warm hearts to embrace the survivors of the holocaust. I expected to be treated with love, understanding, encouragement and desire to help. But the reality was totally different. Some of them told us candidly that had the European Jewry left and made Aliya before the war, the holocaust would not have been so deadly and many Jews would have survived. In contrast to our story of suffering and eventual survival, they described difficult condition in Israel of high unemployment, hunger and constant attacks by the Arabs. I later found that this mentality was indicative of the "old Guard" population that immigrated to Israel before the war. Consequently, the survivors, including myself, vowed not to mention the Holocaust and its tribulations and many internalized our horrific experiences for many years and were ashamed to mention it.

The isolation and indifference the survivors felt from the old-timers, was terribly disappointing. We felt guilty and ashamed for being the victims of the Holocaust. Because of that shame, we internalized the archives of the war years and when we built new homes and started families, continued the silence about the painful subject that haunted us. We carried the pain and severe wound in our souls, deep inside our cores.

The political establishment contributed to the general apathy towards the suffrage of the European Jews. But despite the disappointment and frustration, our dream of fulfilling the Zionist cause stayed intact. The vast majority of the survival community made a gallant effort towards assimilating and fitting into the country. Our contribution encompassed all areas of public life including the military effort, the industrial sector, construction, science and the arts. We, as a whole, were steeped in ideology and a strong belief that only here, Israel, was our place – regardless of the war and difficult conditions. Only recently, our contribution to the successful beginning of the newly born State has been told, recognized and admired. But not all the immigrants accepted the brutal reality of everyday life in Israel during those early years, and many gave up and left the country. Most returned to Germany and again found themselves as refugees waiting for a chance to immigrate to the US or Canada.

Chapter 21

FIRST STEPS

My first assignment was with the Army Corp of Engineers and I reported to its base in the agricultural village of Ramat Hasharon, just north of Tel-Aviv. We lived in a city of tents that were cool during the hot and humid summer months but often collapsed under heavy rains during the winter. My orders were to join a unit whose job was to guard Arab prisoners of war. This activity was tedious and boring and I immediately looked for something else to do. I went to see my commander. He mentioned how impressed he was with my fluent Hebrew and promised to find something else for me. I mentioned during my interview that I held a driver's license issued in Germany and he later suggested for me to be a driver's assistant. The chief driver arranged for a driving test using a British Bedford army pick-up truck with a right side driver seat. I drove with the inspector at my side from Ramat Hasharon to Herzliya with no incidents. But upon returning to the camp, as I made the turn into the camp, I hit the guard booth and the MP barely escaped the careening vehicle. I was court marshaled for destroying military property and was grounded in the camp for several weeks. Staying at the camp was not a big punishment, as I really didn't have anywhere to go or anyone to visit, but it was the end of my driving career. The incident provided endless opportunity for my children, my friends and later my grandchildren to poke fun at my driving adventures.

A chance meeting with the camp's cook, who was one of my recruits at the Dror Kibbutz in Krakow, brought a momentous change in my life. He told me that he and his wife lived in a small apartment in Herzliya and that in his spare time he painted for residential customers with a partner. His partner's wife had a beautiful young sister who was staying with them at Ramat Hasharon and he offered to introduce us. The meeting was to take place at a dance hall in Hertzliya and I joined him with few other soldiers on the agreed evening. We sat, mostly staring at the couples that were dancing, and then he pointed towards a lovely lady that was dancing with another guy. From that first quick glance, I was impressed with her beauty and her strong presence that radiated goodness and strong character. I heard that the gentleman dancing with her had been courting her unwanted for quite some time and that she had tried to terminate their relationship. Knowing that gave me the courage to introduce myself, and I asked her for a dance. We exchanged casual niceties during our dance, and when I escorted her back to her seat I thanked her and said that I enjoyed meeting her and hoped to meet again. During that night, I tossed and turned and could not sleep, thinking about the young lady. Had I fallen in love at first sight? All signs certainly signaled that to be the case. I decided to send her a letter expressing my deep desire to see her again and my growing fondness towards her. I asked the "matchmaker" to hand deliver the letter to its addressee.

Days went by without response and I decided to visit her at her sister's apartment. Feeling very nervous I arrived at the correct address with my heart pounding out of control. I knocked on the door and a pleasant lady holding a baby in her hands opened the door. I knew it must be her sister. She invited me to come in and have a seat and asked me what the purpose of my visit was. I told her about my meeting with her sister at the dance and my desire to see her again. She told me that her name was Edja (Esther in Hebrew) and that her sister Paula was working in a field nearby picking produce. She interrogated me in an open conversation about my past, family and education. The conversation flowed pleasantly and I felt confident that I made a good first impression. I learned from her that Paula arrived in Israel as an orphan with a youth group of Holocaust survivors that were absorbed at the Kibbutz Ramat Yochanan in the north of the country. She was allowed a vacation to help her sister with the birth of her baby son. She then told me about her sister's other suitor and did not hide that fact that she did not approve of that relationship. I returned to the base feeling more confident and determined to pursue the young lady Paula.

At that time my situation at the camp improved significantly when I was put in charge of the camp's snack bar. I moved my bed to the back of the shack and had much free time during the day. In the evenings many young male and female soldiers gathered to buy a soda and mingle. My new conditions were quite an improvement from the crowded tent I just left. I began to make regular visits to the field where Paula worked and always brought her a soda and a chocolate wafer as we exchanged a few words. I remember her wearing a large straw hat guarding her from the intense sun. She wore short pants and a cotton shirt that exposed her hands and legs that were beautifully tanned and resembled the color of chocolate. She looked like a young lady portrayed in a poster of the "Keren Kayemet" organization symbolizing the young healthy generation in the new Israel. My love towards her grew, and, in turn, she treated me with slight indifference mixed with occasional signs of fondness. Nevertheless, our relationship grew stronger, and I visited her any chance I had. Occasionally, late in the evenings, we would go to a dancing hall, dance and meet young folks. When my unit was ordered to move to another site, farther away, we couldn't meet daily, and that separation, filled with anticipation, fueled our love further.

A year and a half later, we decided to get married. But the austere reality and lack of any resources what-so-ever darkened our moment of happiness. Our first worry was where to live. I inquired in the army offices and with the Jewish Agency about housing availability but to no avail. Through friends, I heard about a one bedroom apartment in Jaffa that housed a newcomer family who decided to leave Israel. As a condition to leave the country, they had to relinquish the apartment to an agency that controlled properties previously deserted by Palestinian families. The Army Corps of Engineers provided me with the necessary letter of recommendation and all I needed was to raise the money to purchase the bedroom furniture left by the previous tenant – which I did in a form of a small loan from the Absorption Agency. We then decided on a wedding date – January 3, 1950. We went to a rabbi in Ramat Hasharon to register and after inquiring about my background and my family, we discovered that my grandfather's brother, Rabbi Avram Druskeveitz, was the leader of the Voloshin Yeshiva where this Rabbi studied. But as we got busy with wedding plans, I fell terribly ill and had to be hospitalized. I had severe stomach cramps, could not hold food and lost much weight. When I think now about those days, I can only imagine what Paula had to go through, worrying about her husband to-be with no money, no job prospects, and sick in the hospital. Surely, if she had parents, they would not have approved of this marriage. After two weeks, I was released and the army released me, as it was close to the expiration of my term. I got a job through contacts I had as a guard with the Civil Guard agency which was part of the Tel-Aviv municipality, two months before our wedding date. Prior to our wedding day, I handed invitations to my new co-workers. Later that same day, I received an envelope from the office manager and decided to open, what I thought was a gift, together with my new bride after the wedding.

We chose the Workers Union Hall in Ramat Hasharon for our wedding. Most of the guests were from the bride's side, mostly from Kibbutz Ramat Yochanan with whom Paula came to Israel. After the wedding the group had to walk back to Tel-Aviv to catch the last bus back to the Kibbutz. We danced and sang into early morning hours. Some of the gifts we received included pots & pans, baking pans, ceramic figurines, tableware and a coffee set. We then excitedly opened the envelope from my employer and found that I was given a seven day notice of termination. I will never forget the disappointment and the mean spirited timing of this letter. Needless to say, a honeymoon was not contemplated.

My first job as a civilian in my new country was selling newspapers in a kiosk at the central bus station in Tel-Aviv. The kiosk was located at the heart of the station and I sold to and interacted with thousands of people using the bus system – that was the most popular and affordable mode of transportation at the time. Many of the riders were newcomers from Europe, and I found myself in a hub of human interaction with light conversation and many "shalom" greetings. I was quite shocked, and then embarrassed, to find that I recognized so many faces and sometimes names of people I led during the recruitment period after the war. I felt so ashamed that I was selling papers to many people on whose lives I had such

an impact when I was the Dror Kibbutz leader. I asked to be transferred to another kiosk because of the emotional distress I suffered
and indeed, shortly after, I moved to the Kiosk at the corner of
Allenby and Pinsker streets in the most prestigious section of the
city. There, I sold newspapers and periodicals from around the
world. By contrast to the bus station, my clientele was made of
city officials, poets, members of Knesset – the Israeli Parilament
-(before it was moved to Jerusalem) and ministers in Ben-Gurion's
cabinet. Many would stop to browse and read an article and strike
a conversation with me. Often, my customers remarked with surprise at my excellent Hebrew vocabulary, expecting to hear a typical
broken, heavy accented Hebrew that many newcomers possessed.
I explained with pride that I was educated at the famed Tarbut
School in Vilna. One morning, three leaders form the Labor movement, AaronTzizling, Israel Bar-Yehuda and Bankover stopped to
purchase a paper. I knew the three very well, spending many hours
with them during meetings when they were sent as representatives
of the Yishuv (as we referred to Israel before its statehood) to the
refugee camps in Germany. I didn't think that they would remember me, but one of them asked if my name was Michael and I told
them who I was. They expressed astonishment as to how one of
the leaders of the surviving Jewry in Europe was now selling papers in Tel-Aviv. They reminded me of my achievements in the
camps, my organizational skills, and a talent for public speaking;
they told me that I should immediately report to the Party's office in Tel-Aviv for a job. Indeed with their support I was promptly
given a job as an assistant treasurer of the Tel-Aviv branch of the
Labor Party.

In advance of the coming elections both for the Knesset and
local municipalities, the party sent me to the section which covered

the area of the city that included the streets Sheinkin, Rothschild, Echad H'am and adjoining neighborhoods. My job was to engage in door to door campaigning, delivering election material and asking for the vote. Our section had a list of potential voters, and I spent the mornings at the local headquarters and the evenings – often until very late – knocking on doors and recruiting votes. It was my first encounter with the established, well-to-do class of the Yishuv, who lived in well furnished apartments, which to me seemed palatial, compared to our dilapidated place in Jaffa without electricity, running water, toilet or kitchen. I carry with me to this day some of the extraordinary experiences I encountered while making these house calls. One such encounter was in an apartment on Rothschild Avenue. Immediately, upon getting to the well lit and elegant entrance, I skipped a heart beat thinking to myself, "What am I doing here with the Tel-Aviv aristocracy?" But my curiosity motivated me and I rang the bell. A well dressed man of about 50 opened the door and asked what the purpose of my visit was. I told him that it was probably the wrong address and I turned to leave, but he invited me to stay and offered a cup of tea. I sat there mesmerized and amazed. The living room had expensive and heavy furniture, art on the walls, vases, a well stocked china cabinet, Persian rug and a chandelier fit for a palace. I asked myself, "Am I dreaming? Is that how people live in Eretz Yisrael?" My host recognized my embarrassment, and when I asked how the leftist Labor party got his name as a supporter, he explained that as an importer of raw material, many kibbutzim were his customers. From a purely business perspective he donated money to them, but his ideology, he made clear, was at the other end of the political spectrum.

Another encounter on Rothschild Avenue I remember well. At the entrance to the apartment building I saw a cobbler repairing shoes. I asked him if he knew what floor the person I was look-ing for lived on. He inquired what the purpose of the visit was. I replied that I was with the Labor Party (Achdut H'avoda) and I was there in regards to the elections. He burst into laughter and said, "The person you're looking for is the landlord, a real bourgeoisie and very stingy. Don't waste your time." What's more, he said that person lived in the penthouse apartment (this was before eleva-tors) and that I should save my energy climbing. I went anyway and knocked on the door with hesitation, expecting to be turned down quickly when my political affiliation became clear. To my surprise, he was very friendly and invited me to sit down with him. During the conversation I learned that he was employed by the National Power Company (Chevrat H'chashmal) and lived there alone. The apartment had two bedrooms, a kitchen and toilet and was built as a fifth floor addition on the roof. He then explained how it happened that he became the owner of the building. Together, with other employees of the electrical company, he pur-chased land in the heart of Tel-Aviv secured with loans provided by the employer at favorable rates. That land later became the famed Dizinghoff Square and the track that he and his brother – who also worked for the electrical company – owned what became the site of the Esther movie theatre. With the profits they built the apart-ment building on Rothschild Ave. He then told me that during the British Mandate they were well off because the rent they charged was high. Later, with the establishment of rent control, the tenants were protected and they could hardly afford to pay property taxes. He shared that he was ashamed to admit it, but he could not af-ford to pay for the cleaning and upkeep of the building and did the cleaning himself at night, lest he'd be seen. He then offered me some cognac and sandwiches with imported salami. He said,

"Fellow, sit down and let's enjoy ourselves and talk. As you can see I am lonely and bored." I told him how difficult my absorption in Israel was and how especially challenging our living conditions were without electricity. He was incredulous: "You have no electricity? How could it be that the country could absorb newcomers who volunteered to fight in the war of Independence without providing the bare necessities?" He then promised to call his brother, who was the district manager for the Jaffa region, and arrange for power. Indeed, he kept his promise. In less then two months, they erected electrical poles and our entire alley had light! No more kerosene lamps and smoky rooms. Instead, we had light, and later we purchased a radio. What else could a young couple in the new Jewish state need?

Our good fortunes kept coming, as shortly after, Paula shared with me that she was late in her menstrual cycle and thought that she was pregnant. A visit to the doctor confirmed that she was expecting a child. Our financial and living conditions were still desperate and we did not think that we could provide for a child, so Paula attempted, but did not succeed, to stop the pregnancy. We decided that it was a good sign that perhaps we should have a child. We blessed our fortunes and waited as Paula was beginning to show. She was ashamed of her pregnancy – what an awful period of naivety! She continued to work at the Kitan factory – having to leave early in the morning to catch a couple buses on the way to Herzliya – handling a very noisy and oily weaving machine while breathing cotton dust. These were tough times in the young country and the authorities imposed national austerity called "Tzena," with strict food rations distributed with stamps and providing only for basic nutrition. The milk, diluted with water, was distributed in large jugs and had a blue tint to it. Instead of meat, our only protein was fish filets. There was no limit to the housewife's imagination when it came to cooking variations of the fish. We began to employ all sorts of signs to tell us the sex of the baby, and most indicated that we're going to have a son. Well, on Saturday, the fourth of August 1951 at 10 o'clock in the morning, we had our first born, a baby girl. We named her Chaya, after my mother who was killed in the holocaust. The baby was beautiful and as she grew, she had gorgeous light curls and looked like a child in an advertisement. We received a baby stroller from friends, as was the custom at the time, and were expected to hand it down later to another needy couple. Against bad spirits, we tied a red string on both sides of the stroller, just to be on the safe side. I was forced to stop my work for the party because of financial reasons – it was considered a privilege to actually pay wages to the believers in the socialistic left, and I did not get paid for two months. Paula had to quit after delivering the baby and our situation was dire.

Paula and Michael, Ramat Ha'Sharon 1948

Paula and Michael's wedding photo January 3 1950

Chapter 22

GETTING SETTLED

I succeeded in getting a part-time job as an assistant in the book-keeping department of a private company, The Central Company for Commerce and Investments, whose offices resided at 39 Lilin-bloom Street in the financial district of Tel-Aviv. As the saying goes, "there's nothing more permanent than the temporary", my part-time job with the firm lasted twenty years and, after the merger with the Clal Concern, another twenty years. The Central Co. was founded in 1944 by fourteen building supplies merchants, land owners and financiers, with the purpose of forming a partnership to purchase half of the Nesher cement plant in Haifa. The other half was bought by Solel Boneh and the Chevrat Ha'ovdim. The sharp switch from political activities to the private sector was quite a culture shock. The decorum at the company was formal and correct. Most wore suits and ties and I felt that I was back in Europe. The leadership was composed of mostly highly educated German Jews who spoke with a particular accent and had extensive careers in banking and mercantile.

As a part-timer, my initial wage was 45 Lira per month, and I worked hard with focused dedication and a deep desire to succeed. After 90 days, I was told that I could continue and my wage would increase to 60 Lira, retroactive to my first day. When I got that paycheck, with the increase in pay, we felt that we had just received a small fortune, and we dreamed of ways to spend the money. We decided on a dining room table and chairs, which was a big improvement from the wooden box we used as an eating surface. The condition of the apartment and lack of basic sanitary conditions made life difficult and adversely influenced the baby's development. She fell seriously ill, and ran an extremely high fever. Our concern led us to the best pediatrician we could find in Tel-Aviv. He ordered quick tests and found that she had an infection originated from mice typhus. Only a strong antibiotic that required special permission from the Health Ministry would save the child's life. When the medicine arrived neither one of us could make Chaya swallow the liquid and we stood there totally helpless crying together until our neighbor who was older and more experience helped with the situation. Within 24 hours there was an improvement and, a week later, a complete recovery.

Following Chaya's improvement, the engineers representing the housing authorities, ruled that we must evacuate our dwelling for repairs because it was unsafe and might collapse at any time; alternative housing was not being offered and we had no idea where to go. I heard from friends I met at the DP camp in Germany that a new neighborhood was being built in the Kiryat Shaul area. I went there to inquire and found that indeed an apartment complex was developed for members of the Progressive Party (which no longer exists). Despite my previous political affiliation, they agreed to sign me up, and I purchased a one bedroom unit. The price was 1800 Lira with 1/3 due in advance and the remainder upon completion of the construction. They allowed me some time to sell the lease of our Jaffa apartment in order to come up with the down payment. The buyer we found insisted on immediate occupation and according to the developers, our new unit would be ready in two months time. My wife's sister agreed to host us and the three of us crowded in her two bedroom apartment in Ramat Ha'Sharon. Every day that went by was a struggle for our hosts, with their two children, as well as for us. I decided to go to the construction site to inquire about the progress and to see if it might be possible to move in prior to completion. At the site, several buildings were standing; some had occupants in them already and others were not yet finished. I asked the project manager to take me to our unit so I could assess if it was suitable for habitation and he told that they hadn't started our building yet. "It's impossible sir," I said, "You must have made a mistake. I already paid the required down payment and my family and I are living temporarily based on the promise of two months. Are we going to be homeless?" Our Jaffa apartment was sold. We already paid the money to the developer and it was inconceivable that we extend our stay with my sister in law. I decided to quickly go to the developer's office and, until I arrived there, I was still convinced that the project manager made a simple mistake and that my agony was in vain. In the office I asked for the partners whom I met originally. When they saw me their faces projected bad news; they lowered their eyes and said not a word. I yelled, "What is happening here? I just got here from the construction site and was told that you didn't start my building." They tried to calm me down, explaining that they stumbled on difficulties with the project and that, with an additional 1000 Lira; they might let us have a completed unit that was larger then what we purchased. I told them that there was no chance that I could accept their proposal, as I could hardly manage to raise the rest of the money I owed for the original apartment. "How could you have taken from me the only money I have to my name and promised we could take possession in two months? Now we have no place to live and no money." I lost control of myself and started to tussle with them physically and they ran away from the office. Other office workers that witnessed what was happening sat me down, brought me water and tried to calm me down.

My wife Paula was in total shock when I told her that our attempt to purchase a home failed completely. We pondered what to do, realizing that we could not extend our stay with Paula's sister, Edja. We then made up our minds. Our only choice was to invade one of the units and become squatters. We located a unit that seemed suitable on the ground floor of one of the buildings: the walls already built, floors had been poured, but there were no windows, doors, water or electricity. We took advantage of the Shavuot holiday knowing that there would be no construction, hired a person with a horse and a flat bed carriage and at dusk invaded the unit. We lit a kerosene lamp and that drew the attention of the site's guard. We knew that he would quickly notify the owners of our invasion. Other tenants who lived nearby came to inquire, and when they saw a mother holding a baby – both crying – they offered help. They gave us food and water and invited us to use their bathrooms and shower. That first night was a sleepless night and the next morning a large group of neighbors gathered around us with encouragement and support reassuring us that we were on the right side of the law and that the unscrupulous developers took advantage of us. They brought us blankets to cover the windows and one of the neighbors had an extra door we used to cover the open entrance. We were overwhelmed with the show of warmth and support and it lifted our spirits and resolve.

The next morning the police arrived with an evacuation warrant. We refused to leave and they began to move in with a show of force. Paula and I started to scream and then the baby began to cry. All the neighbors showed up, men women and children and made a human circle around us. A few of the men confronted the cops and told them that blood would be shed if we were touched. The Sergeant radioed his superiors at the police station in Ramat-Gan and received instructions to leave the mother and baby but to arrest me. The cops took me to the station and put me in a cell. The next morning an officer took me for questioning and asked me to consider legal representation. Shortly after returning to the cell one of the developers, along with an attorney, came with a proposal to release me immediately if I agreed to voluntarily evacuate the apartment within two weeks. I refused arguing that I would still be homeless in two weeks with no real options. They came back with another offer which provided us with temporary housing until our unit was completed. I agreed to these terms, and when I returned to my family I was surprised to see that the house was still surrounded by our neighbors, protecting Paula and the baby. Everyone erupted in spontaneous celebration to mark our victory. Despite major difficulties, we had a little corner for ourselves, even though it had no doors or windows. To our surprise, the water was connected and we had a functioning faucet in the kitchen. But it was a short lived truce. After a couple of days a person came by presenting himself as the rightful owner of our apartment. As it turned out, the developer transferred the apartment to a plumbing sub-contractor. The owner spoke calmly and showed some solidarity with our predicament. He explained that he just sold the unit to another family. They were planning to move in within few days and we needed to leave. My step-uncle Joseph heard of the situation. He told us not to move and that he would provide us with private guards while I was at work. For a period of a week, my wife and baby were protected by three strong men, which allowed me to go back to work where I was still newly employed and not at all sure of any permanent status and a secure roof over our heads. Later I found that the threat was a ploy to scare us and make us leave the premises. The situation became unbearable with no resolution in sight, with anxious, sleepless nights and days at work disconnected from reality. The despair caused me to lose my hair as I discovered one morning while shaving that a large clump had fallen from the middle of my scalp.

My superiors noticed my absent-mindedness and understood that I was under duress. One executive, Dr. Fritz Neumann, who was from the Jewish German aristocracy, frequently inquired about my wellbeing and the progress of my absorption, asked me how I was doing. I told him about our invading the apartment and the threat of evacuation unless we came up with additional 1,000 Lira which we did not have for the larger unit. He promised to think about our situation and inquire if he'd be able to assist us. Needless to say, we counted the hours, the days and the nights, waiting to hear back from Dr. Neumann. When I could wait no longer, I went to see my boss to ask if he had any news for us. "Come in," he said, "What took you so long? You know how busy and unorganized I am and I meant to speak to you for days about a plan to help you." He took a piece of paper to scribble on and asked me, "What is the cost of the unit the developers are offering you?" "2,200 Lira," I said. "And how much have you already paid?" "600 Lira." "So you need 1,600 Lira," he said and wrote the amount down. He then told me that the company would help us using a special fund of government resources: 45 tons of cement and 1200 Kg of steel, the value of which translated to 1800 Lira in the black market. These supplies were transferred to the developers in exchange for our new apartment. We moved in at last. To this day, I remember the contribution and generosity of Dr. Neumann and the company's executive staff, without which we would not have our own place.

Chapter 23

BUILDING A CAREER

The activities of the firm developed beyond its original scope of manufacturing and selling cement and with the wave of development that the young country experienced, the Central Company was involved with the funding of and investing in various enterprises. I moved from the bookkeeping department to the Treasury and found satisfaction and interest in my work. The Company invested heavily in funding and acquiring manufacturing plants, including Kitan textile, Samson Tires, Urdan Pladot (metal fabrication), Akrilan, Coca Cola bottling, Neshr cement plants in Ramlah and Beit Shemesh and the paper plant of Hadera. In the finance field, we acquired a private bank, Bank Artzie, became partners in an export bank, a Swiss-Israeli bank, and opened a branch in Brussels called "Centrada." In time I became the company's Treasurer and was responsible for a wide range of activities, both at home and abroad. We also managed the financial matters of the textile cartel in Israel which involved seven companies. I developed relationships with financial institutions and the Finance Ministry that improved the company's liquidity, which gave me personal gratification as well as improved my standing with the leadership of the company. It felt as if I came a long way since my days as a junior bookkeeper, having to ask my superiors to endorse remittances. In the early fifties the head of the company was Mr. Aaron Netanel, who was engaged in many activities and was also the President of the worldwide Macabbi Games. After his death, the late Mr. Avraham Friedman – who was one of the founders of the car manufacturer Keiser Ilan – arrived from Haifa. Alongside him was one of the chieftains of Israel commerce and finance, the late Gershon Gourewitz. I mention all of them with fondness and admiration as I owe them my development and understanding of world views, business acumen and public relations, all of which anchored my growth and success. My immediate supervisor of twenty years, Mr. David Svirski, was my mentor and trusted ally, not least because of our shared roots in Vilna.

On May 8, 1956 our son Yossi was born. To have a son following a girl was a true blessing. Chaya was five years old when he was born and accepted her brother with joy and love. We named him after our two lost fathers as Yossef Leib, and to this day my son signs his first name and middle name as was given to him. The task of running the household and raising the children was entirely my wife's. With no outside help what-so-ever, she raised them to be healthy in body and mind. Unfortunately, there were no grandparents to spoil the kids and perhaps that was one of the reasons why they were obedient and disciplined. My wife Paula deserves all the credit for keeping the family together, as I was a father for weekends only. I worked very hard to earn a living and improve our conditions and at times had to take a second job and work overtime.

In the early seventies, the Central Co. experienced a leadership crisis. The founding generation either passed away or was too ill to function. Gerson Gourewitz had a stroke and became paralyzed, Avraham Friedman had a heart attack and David Svirski took over the Swiss-Israel bank and relocated to Europe. The void was filled by the second generation of the founders who changed the culture of the company. It became less professional, filled with personal ambitions, infighting and ultimately deteriorated. Behind the scenes, negotiations took place to merge the Central Co. with Clal Israel Co. Clal was a dynamic company whose CEO Mr. Aaron Dovrat was energetic and talented. The chief matchmaker behind the merger was the minister of finance, Mr. Pinchas Sapeer, who was one of the Clal's founders. With the merger, the associates received assurance in writing, securing five years employment and the same benefits, which were considered at the time most advanced in the country. Avraham Friedman became the co-CEO with Aaron Dovrat in the combined company. I was offered and refused a position as deputy treasurer of Clal and consequently for a period of one and a half years was stuck with no specific title. During that same period, I became involved also with financing the imports of Grundig electronics from Germany and the Candi appliance Corporation from Italy. The importer was the late Moshe Ben-Shaul who was a sharp businessman and a kind man. I accompanied him on business trips to both countries. During 1965, while still with the Central Co., I had the opportunity to combine a business trip to Europe with a family visit to the United States. The trip was authorized by the management and I felt confident of my position with the firm. My first stop was Germany where I met with the top managers from the Grundig Corporation, including its founder and president Mr. Max Grundig. From Germany I went to Brussels to visit the Centrada bank. My reception there was exceptional, being picked up at the airport by a chauffer who followed me for two days, and staying at the most expensive hotel in the city. In the evenings, the bank manager and his lieutenants took me to some of the best restaurants and entertainment clubs in Brussels. This was their reward for my contribution to the success and growth of the bank. Then I traveled to London for a visit with my good friend the late Arieh Friedman who was the El-Al station manager in London. The next destination was the US. I wanted to attend a wedding that took place in Minneapolis knowing that I would meet many family members there. But first, I went to New York, where I stayed with my aunt Deborah Rose from my father's side. I also met an uncle from my mother's side that came from Philadelphia. Another uncle from my mother's side lived in Los Angeles, but I did not get to see him. At my cousin's wedding, I met dozens of cousins and relatives who came from all over the US. They went out of their way to make sure I was welcomed and fought over who would host me at their house. (These relatives or their descendents left Eastern Europe to North America during the period of atrocities aimed at the Jews called Pogroms at the beginning of the twentieth century). For two months I traveled and I left my wife Paula at home with our two children. I could only imagine how difficult it was for her and know very few women who would let their husbands go for such a long period.

Back to the Clal period in Israel. The industrial activities of the concern were managed by the Clal-Industry division. During the 1975 reorganization, a decision was made to de-centralize and each division was to be run independently. I was offered and accepted the Finance Manager position. The President of the division was Mr. Tzvi Tzoor, "Tchera", who was the Israel Defense Forces' Chief of Staff and later Deputy Defense Minister under Mr. Shimon Peres. His deputy was Mr. Meir Shani and I was given the challenge of building the financial structure of the division from the ground up. Mr. Tzoor's management philosophy was that we – as the division support office – provided the training, consulting and oversight, while each of the plants reporting to us was responsible for their own accounting and cash management. I had a different point of view and made the case that in order for us to have leverage with the banks when negotiating credit terms, we should pull our finances together. In a sentence, my argument was "the sum of the whole had more power then its parts separately." Furthermore, I didn't think that we would be successful in pressuring the units to cooperate without showing them tangible benefits. During a series of meetings with the CFO's of the plants, I presented the plan for cooperation. I would establish a financial clearinghouse – an exchange – that would absorb the liquidity of all the units, garnering better interest rates then the rates they would have received, and in turn extend loans back to the units, as the need arose, at better rates then offered by the market. My exchange did not operate with profit as a motive, and because of the volume of cash at my disposal, I was able to command superior interest rates and low fee structure from the banks. The cooperation with the plants continued to develop and flourish as they realized the extent of the benefits offered to them by our own "private bank." In time I was able to leverage the financial power of the entire division and negotiated terms with the Internal Tax Administration, Social Security, the retirement funds and the utility companies, which allowed for us to pay as one unit for the dozens of plants, in exchange for better credit terms free of interest. These institutions preferred a single payer that paid on time and that synergy worked well for all sides.

The scope of the financial activities grew rapidly and later included transactions in foreign currencies. We established contacts with banks abroad. At the beginning, our conduits were Israeli banks who already established beachheads in both Europe and the US. As the demand for foreign currency grew due to the growing import and export activities, I eventually established direct relationships with the foreign banks. Because of strict Israeli banking regulations and rapid inflation at the time, foreign money was tight and very expensive. Consequently, there was high demand for foreign credit. I traveled to Europe and was successful in opening credit lines with a few leading banks. The credit lines I secured were short term, and as collateral we used the income from our export business. The activities became so large and time consuming that it became increasingly difficult to manage from afar. We began to evaluate the need for a permanent European office. It was natural for me, as the person who developed these relationships, to manage that effort. It was decided that Frankfurt, as the European financial center, would be a suitable place. We already had a marketing office there representing ICI and the Kitan textile plants, and that center would help us at the beginning. In one of the exploration trips to Frankfurt, I suffered a heart attack and following the hospitalization period, was forbidden to fly for additional two months. Upon my return to Israel, I slowed my work schedule and the plans for opening the European office were put on hold.

Paula, Michael, Chaya & Yossi Ramat-Gan, 1959

Chaya's Bat-Mitzvah Tel-Aviv, 1963

Yossi's Bar-Mitzvah Tel-Aviv, 1969

Chapter 24

RETURNING TO EUROPE

Slowly I began returning to full health and normal activities and in May of 1987 decided that I was ready for my mission abroad. We left for Frankfurt in August 1987 and during the four years there the scope of my activities there grew markedly. The banks there offered us tens of millions of dollars in credit at very good terms. I used these sources to finance the imports of raw material to our factories. In return, the revenues from our exports also funneled through the same banking channels. These relationships allowed us to raise funds in a five year cycle. We negotiated similar deals three times, and in total, raised approximately 30 million dollars for our division. The liquidity and relative low cost of borrowing, in comparison to terms available in Israel, changed the financial condition of our plants for the better and improved their bottom line. Aside from the success in business, we developed our social network and visited many places in the Continent. We also hosted numerous visitors from Israel, many of whom were colleagues from Clal.

During my tenure in Frankfurt, several developments took place at our headquarters in Tel-Aviv. Replacing the division president Mr. Amos Mar Chaim was Mr. Moshe Schteingart. He came to our division from the commerce division of Clal. They had a subsidiary based in Rotterdam, Holland that dealt with shipping containers and trading petroleum products. The company suffered heavy losses over the years, and later it was discovered that lucrative commissions were not unusual. I knew for a long time that Mr. Schteingart was eyeing the company I was running in Frankfurt, Ikatex, which was profitable to combine it with the Dutch subsidiary that was losing money. There were also changes with the ownership of Clal, with Bank Hapoalim selling it to the Discont group of the Rekanati family. With that came the retirement of our long time CEO Mr. Aaron Dovrat, a top executive Yitzhak Sharem and many other senior managers.

As I was approaching retirement age, I considered ending my stay in Europe. Contributing to this was also the stabilization of the Israeli economy, lowering of the inflation rate and the fact that the interest rates for foreign credit declined to levels similar to that of the banks abroad. I returned to Tel-Aviv to discuss the terms of my retirement with Mr. Aaron Dovrat, Amos Sapir and Chezi Dovrat. The subject could not be delayed, as it was not to my advantage to negotiate – after employment of 40 years – with a new team of executives who "did not know Joseph." As it is typical in most negotiations, the parties must compromise. Even though I did not get all I wanted and thought I deserved according to similar situations, I agreed to the terms offered to me by the Clal managers. It was decided that I would continue managing Ikatex in Frankfurt for six more months following my retirement date of September 1991. With my retirement and closure of the office, I decided to take advantage of my relationships and knowledge I acquired over the years and attempt to make a go of it alone. I rented an apartment which was also my office and hired a part time assistant. In October of 1991 we returned to our Ramat Gan home at Churgin Street. My son-in-law Pini Maor who was a partner in a company that had an office in Germany, allowed me to use a room there as needed. In the year and a half of independent activities,

I realized how difficult it was to get established without the backing of a well capitalized organization. In addition, the frequent trips to Germany took a physical toll. I closed my Frankfurt office and switched my focus to financial consulting and brokering. The European bankers I knew helped me to the best of their ability, and to this day, as most of them have retired, I continue to correspond and stay in touch.

Clal office, Frankfurt 1988

Chapter 25

NEVER FORGET

With the closing of the chapter of my financial and business career, I started to devote most of my time to the Association of The Survivors of Vilna and Vicinity, the Central Fund for the Holocaust Research and other organizations.

Our lives were illuminated by wonderful and uplifting moments. In August of 1963, our daughter Chaya was Bat Mitzvahed in Tel-Aviv with hundreds of guests, family and friends as well as colleagues from work. The Bar-Mitzvah of our son Yossi in May of 1969 had a sequence of events, including a Tfilin ceremony at the Western Wall in Jerusalem, Aliyah to the Torah at the Great Synagogue of Ramat-Gan and a banquet for over 400 guests. At the first night of Chanukah, 1971, we gave the hand of our daughter under the Chupah to Pinchas (Pini) Machtei and the ceremony was officiated by Rabi Lau. To accommodate the crowd of 600 guests, we had to rent the three halls of the Gilton banquet center. The arrival of Chaya and Pini's first child, Liron, at the eve of the Shavuot celebration, was a momentous occasion, marking the birth of our first grandchild and great-grandchild (from the Machtei side). A few years later Dana was born, and after years of trying to produce a son, they "succeeded" and gave birth to a third girl Yael. Our son Yossi Leib who left to the United States to study, established himself there, got married to Cathy Surratt and they gave birth to their daughter Ella. We are now delighted and proud to have four granddaughters, each one so unique and beautiful in her own way. Liron, our oldest granddaughter who married Yigal Perlmutter, gave birth to our great-grandson Matan in March of 2004.

We are not getting any younger and age reminds us of how fragile we are. A big part of every day is now dedicated to staying healthy, visiting doctors and managing our medications. We have plenty of idle time which we use to stay in touch with friends and family. With our son who lives with his family in the US, we stay in touch with weekly phone calls, letters and an annual visit. Our daughter followed her husband to England for few years for a career opportunity and that separation was very difficult. She returned to Israel when our granddaughter Yael joined the military.

To summarize my life's journey to date, it must be said that the happiness, satisfaction and friendship between my wife and I, and among our children and grandchildren, brought uplifting joy after my early years of darkness. I thank God for all the goodness and grace that he bestowed on me and hope that the future would only bring blessings and joy. Most important to me is to grow old gracefully with clarity of mind and good health. I wish for the day that the Israeli people will – at long last – live in peace and the nation who struggled for survival for so long will find its serenity.

Vilna's House, Tel-Aviv

Vilna's House, Tel-Aviv

Vilna's House, Tel-Aviv

Paula and Michael, in front of childhood apartment, Vilna 1993

Third of May Street, Vilna 1993

*Ponar Memorial, 50 year commemoration of the
Ghetto's annihilation, 1993*

H.K.P survivors, Darmstadt, Germany 2005 honoring Major Plage'

ROOTS

In writing about my family history, I encounter difficulties which are typical to the generation of survivors. Nothing survived to help the research. The photographs and letters that were kept for posterity from one generation to another were destroyed with their keepers. My effort therefore was focused on relatives in Israel and abroad. In researching my mother's side, Zalman Gordon was most helpful and indeed he collected information spanning four generations. The details regarding my father's family I was able to go back only three generations.

The Schochot Roots

My mother's grandfather, Rabbi Faivel Margalit Gordon was born around the year 1800. He was the Rabbi of the Slobotka (a suburb of Kovno) in Lita, unfortunately I could not find the name of his wife. The Rabbi and his wife had four sons and one daughter. Only one son kept the name Gordon, Shalom Zalman, and the rest were given other names: Yehuda Goldberg, Chanoch Gides, Avraham Drooskovitz and Meir Shochot, my mother's father. The daughter's name was Chaya Sarah.

The practice of giving sons a "fake" last name was a ploy to avoid conscription. According to the Czarist Russia, a single son was not to be called to serve.

Of all Rabbi Gordon's children, only Avraham Drooskovitz was murdered brutally by the Lithuanians during a pogrom against the Jews in Kovno. The other boys and the girl either migrated abroad or died prior to the Holocaust.

My grandfather Meir Shochot and my grandmother Feiga Mera had three sons, Faivel, Yechiel and Abba and one daughter my mother Chaya Sarah. Faivel and Yechiel immigrated to America at the turn of the century and Abba with his wife Feiga and their only daughter Sarah perished in the Holocaust. My grandfather Rabbi Meir Shochat left his parents house and arrived in Vilna before WWI. Despite his ordination as Rabbi, he turned to commerce, traded in flour successfully. During the war years of 1914 to 1918 many thousands died of starvation but Rabbi Meir always had food and helped others. My grandfather searched for a proper match for his daughter Chaya and was willing to offer a sizable dowry. The designated groom was my father Leib Schemiavitz. A large wedding took place in the early 1920's. My grandfather Meir Shochot died in September 1939 few days after the break of WWII and my widowed grandmother came to live with us. She was murdered during the "Yellow Sheinim" Action. My maternal uncle Abba had a grocery store at the building where we lived and owned. He and his wife worked endlessly but made a good living from the store which was located in and frequented by high income clientele. They too had an apartment in our building.

The Schemiavitz Roots

The Schemiavitz family is from the hamlet of Shirvint, in the province of Vulkomeer (Ukemarge) in Lita. My father Leib was the youngest son of my grandfather Shmuel Michael and my grandmother Leah Golda. My father had five sisters, Chaya, Canda, Deborah, Rivkah and Rishkah and two brothers, Yirmiyahu Shlomo and Yitzhak Yaakov. With the exception of his sister Rivkah who died in the Holocaust, the other sisters migrated to America at the turn of the century. The three brothers died in the Holocaust.

My grandfather Shmuel Micahel had a tavern with an official alcoholic beverage permit. A private brewing company hired him to be the region's representative. The beer arrived in barrels and was stored and bottled for retail consumption in a cellar to keep temperatures low. He was also involved in leasing land with fruit orchards from landowners. My grandmother Leah Golda raised the large family and according to my father was a righteous and generous person who had a big heart and was always willing to help the less fortunate. Her oldest son, Yirmiyahu Shlomo, who was known to be especially brilliant and possessed broad interests, looked for a better future beyond Shirvint and move to Vilna. He got involved in the lumber business, which was mostly owned by Jews, using his knowledge of forestry. In Shirvint, the family's matriarch's Leah Golda passed away and my widowed grandfather remarried a much younger divorcee with two young children. Despite his advanced age, the newly wed had a son whose name was Yossef (Yossi) who carried the last name Schemiavitz. My grandfather died in Shirvint and prior to the beginning of hostilities of WWI in 1914, the Russians cleared the Jewish population from the German border accusing them of collaboration with the German enemy. Vilna's Jews were saved from this decree and my father escaped Shirvint and arrived in Vilna.

The Russian army suffered severe losses in the battlefield and the Germans conquered large swats of land including Vilna. The Jewish population welcomed the Germans after years of abuse and pogroms by the Russians. The German army confiscated the food warehouses, clothing centers, lumber and coal, building their inventory for the winter. My father was a strong and courageous fellow and plotted to escape back to Shirvint to smuggle food and supplies back to starving Vilna. That was a dangerous enterprise having to cut through the German lines but the knowledge of every forest trail between the village and the large city enabled him to make many successful trips. My uncle Yirmiyahu sold the merchandise for gold coins and accumulated a small fortune. The end of the war brought seismic political changes to Europe with crumbled empires who controlled many nations, making it possible for these new countries to rise out of the ruins including among them independent Poland and Lita. According to the peace conference in Versailles Vilna was annexed with the newly independent Lita and became its capitol. Poland which ruled Vilna for twenty years did not accept the Versailles accord and invaded the city.

My father and his older brother Yirmiyahu took advantage of the economic downturn and purchased real estate properties, forest land and a wood mill. Uncle Yirmiyahu married an aristocratic lady named Chaya tova and dad continued to live with the childless couple. Later, my father married a lady form the Shochot family. It was a match made between two prominent families, one with a rabbinical lineage and the other well to do merchants. Using the dowry money and some of his own, my father started a beer brewing business and later in partnership with the Segal brothers (who migrated to Israel in the 1930's and started a winery there that is still there) a winery and separately also a part in a grain mill. The crash of the American stock market in 1929 and the following global depression had a big impact on the economy and dad's businesses collapsed and he returned to help his brother manage the real estate in Vilna. His holdings included full ownership in a large apartment building and partnership in two other properties. Father's responsibilities included collecting rent, supervising the repairs and upkeep. He received a salary, a share of the profits and we had an apartment to live in including all expenses. We lived a comfortable and secure middle class existence. Uncle's Yirmiyahu's wife Chaya Tova passed away in 1929 while vacationing in the exclusive Karlsbad Czechoslovakia. I was only three years old at the time and have little memories of her. From stories told, I gathered that her funeral was attended by many people including many civic organizations who were the beneficiaries of her diversified philanthropic work. After her death, my uncle married a widow named Sonya Kooriski who had two sons Music and Moola.

Paula and Michael 2004

Chaya and Yossi, 2006

Chaya, Yossi, Cathy and Ella, Charlotte

Chaya with Liron, Yigal and great grandson Matan, Israel

Michael's 80th birthday, standing to Michael's right, Paula, granddaughters: Yael, Liron & Donna and Chaya. In front are: Yigal Perlmutter, Pini Maor

Made in the USA
Columbia, SC
15 August 2023

21690849R00122